The Handspinner's Guide to Selling

The *Handspinner's* Guide to Selling

by Paula Simmons

Pacific Search Press

Pacific Search Press, 222 Dexter Avenue North,
    Seattle, Washington 98109
© 1979 by Paula Simmons. All rights reserved
Printed in the United States of America

Edited by Betsy Rupp Fulwiler
Designed by Paula Schlosser

Library of Congress Cataloging in Publication Data

Simmons, Paula.
   The handspinner's guide to selling.

   Bibliography: p.
   Includes index.
   1. Handicraft—Marketing.   2. Hand spinning.
I.   Title.
HD2341.S55   658.89′677   79-12490
ISBN 0-914718-45-2

Contents

Acknowledgments

My thanks go to Levi Ross and Noel Rockwell for providing equipment plans and drawings, and to Lorraine Wells and Jennifer Gottdiener for generously sharing details of their equipment. Ruth Richardson deserves special thanks, not only for the many photographs that she herself took, but also for the many others that she printed and enlarged in preparation for this book.

Preface

However new you are to spinning, you have probably considered the possibility of selling your work, and even speculated on the potential market and the problems that might be encountered. It is my hope that by passing along what my husband and I have learned during many years of spinning for a living, you will see that there are really no insurmountable obstacles.

In a way, this book is a companion to *Spinning and Weaving with Wool*, my first spinning book, which gives instruction in spinning techniques and also shows a wide range of available spinning wheels. Both texts are designed as reference guides, either to be read from the beginning or opened up to particular subjects. So that chapters can be rather self-contained, there is some repetition of a few important bits of information that are relevant to more than one chapter.

There will be times when, for the sake of brevity, I will refer to your product as "yarn," but in most instances this can be taken to mean handspun yarn and/or the products made from it, such as woven, knitted, or crocheted items. Also, when I use the word "craftsman," no specific gender is intended—it is written for both.

I am writing here for all handspinners who want to sell their yarn. The excitement of selling is to watch your production capabilities grow and marketing opportunities open up, so that you can do successfully as much as you would like to do.

Selling can be a reason to do more of what you enjoy doing most.

Blessed is he who has found his work;
let him ask no other blessedness.

Carlyle

Production

The one thing indispensable to a livelihood from handspinning is a system for turning out the work. Production, unlike selling, can be a very private thing—whether or not you get the work done is entirely your own problem.

Speed

The best time to start selling is before you are a fast spinner. The advantage of selling while you are slow is that your orders will be coming in slowly at first. If they do come in a little faster than you can fill them, it is still encouraging, for you can see that all you have to do is become faster, and you will be making more money.

Speed comes only through practice, and although you will not be making much per hour at first, it is nice to get paid for practicing. Also, the need to fill orders will mean that more time will be spent spinning, which will result in greater skill. The very fact of spinning for sale will make you conscious of the need to increase speed in order to make a fair wage. In working for speed, avoid any hand technique that cannot be speeded up, such as the "inchworm" way of spinning. (Techniques and habits conducive to faster spinning are covered in the "Speed Spinning" chapter of *Spinning and Weaving with Wool*.)

In order to maintain a certain consistent speed, you will learn to overlook the occasional seed or irregularity. The temptation is to slow down in order to tidy up the yarn, but it is better to spin the wool as it comes,

once it is carded, if production is important. What is desirable is the look and feel of handspun. It is also generally agreed that impeccably spun yarn does not always sell well.

Undue importance has been given to the number of *yards* a person is able to spin per hour. Although it is an obvious gauge of spinning speed, it does not relate to the reality of selling. Yarn is usually sold by weight instead of by yardage, and yarn buyers are accustomed to purchasing it that way. The raw materials for spinning are also sold by weight. So it is the actual *weight* of the yarn that you spin per hour, of the size or sizes you sell, that can help you decide when you are spinning fast enough to be selling profitably.

As your spinning speed increases, you may feel a need for a faster spinning wheel. Shop for a wheel that not only has a high drive ratio, but also can be used with minimum effort. If you are exhausted by three hours of fast spinning, then a slower person can outproduce you. The wheel must also be suited for the kind of yarn you are producing, with the orifice and hook size compatible with the yarn size, and a bobbin of sufficient length to accommodate the amount of yarn you want to have in one skein. ("Spinning Wheels" at the end of the "Equipment" chapter has more suggestions about buying a spinning wheel.)

Unless limited by your technique or your equipment, actual spinning speed depends on: (1) the kind and quality of wool; (2) the amount of contamination by seeds,

burrs, and dirt; (3) the type and thoroughness of carding; (4) the type or size of yarn being spun; and (5) the amount of twist in the yarn.

Spinning of the yarn, however, is only a small part of the work involved in making yarn for sale, and it is necessary to view production in its larger perspective when considering speed. Faster spinning can be an eventual goal, while efficiency in the rest of the operation (for example, wool washing, carding, yarn blocking, packing and wrapping orders) is something that could be achieved even sooner, once the need is recognized.

Efficiency

To make the most out of your wool processing time, wash fleeces in large quantities, allowing them to soak while you go about your other work. If you weave, wind several warps while you are at it. It pays to size your warp chains in larger quantities, for it takes nearly as much time and effort to size a few as it does to size many. Also, the more chains you have, the more latitude you have in designing your warps.

If possible, leave wool-washing equipment, warping reel, packing and mailing supplies, and other such things set up and ready to use. Much time and initiative can be spent in putting things away and getting them out again.

Organizing your work area to save time and steps also can allow you to get more spinning done. For instance, have enough pairs of scissors and other often needed small items around so that you do not spend time looking for them whenever you need them. (If you buy extras, remember that they are a legitimate business expense.) Have as much of your supplies and equipment as possible in one room or in adjoining rooms to save running all over the house when you are trying to complete an order. Consolidation of your working area into one part of the house is also important when claiming business deductions for heat, electricity, and house space used.

If a certain amount of time must be spent in cooking for your family, consider preparing large enough quantities for several meals. This would save you enough time to spin a considerable amount of extra yarn each week. I find that the need to organize my time has resulted in better planned menus. By bringing a wheel into the kitchen, spinning can even be done while meals are cooking.

Perfecting each process, such as the wool washing or sizing of handspun warps, to a point where it is handled *routinely* will also save time. The advantage of any system is that you can just go ahead and do it, without thinking.

Another kind of system is the sharing of chores with family or friends, not only on a social basis, but also for mutual help. This can be done by sharing work, such as sizing warps; by sharing equipment, such as a drum carder; or by taking individual responsibility for certain parts of the processing. At our house, for example, my husband

Over sixty chains of natural colored handspun warp, sized and drying. (By Ross and Paula Simmons)

washes and cards the fleeces, we both spin the yarn for our own warps, I spin the customer yarn orders and our weft yarn, he washes and blocks all the yarn, I do the paper work, and so on. It is easier to take up where someone else left off, or know that at a certain point someone else will take over, than to carry the whole load yourself. Working with someone else who is as determined as you are is also a good way to make money with your spinning. And making money is one clear way of gauging your own progress. One note of caution though: avoid any arbitrary division of labor. Invariably one person can do some things more easily than the other person can, which means that with a little luck, each is able to get out of doing the job he or she least wants to do. There is nothing like job satisfaction to boost production.

Specialty

Speed and efficiency in production are useful, but only if you are able to achieve your goal of selling what you produce. To work up a following of customers who recognize your work, it helps to have a product that is distinctly your own creation. A specialty could feature black sheep shades, vegetable dyed colors, or high quality chemically dyed handspun. It could be exotic fibers, linen, synthetics, or custom spinning of dog hair. It could be a yarn type, such as multiple-ply, highly textured yarn, extremely bulky yarn, or extremely fine yarn. It also could be certain articles made from your yarn, or just a way of labeling or packaging.

If you do specialize in a certain type of yarn or product, choose one that you like doing, for once you become known for it, this will comprise the bulk of your orders. It may become a bit dull, however profitable, if it is something you do not enjoy. Also, in order to be able to do it indefinitely, it has to fit into your working conditions—your space, time, and access to materials.

The fact of specialization can become a recommendation for your yarn. Like the specialist in almost any field, the longer you specialize the more skillful you become, and the more confidence the customer has in your product. Keep in mind that successful work of almost any nature usually expresses itself in an economy of technique and style. Anything overdone reveals confusion or ambivalence. The more certain you are of what you are doing, the more your work reflects your confidence. In wine it is what is called "authority," and it is what people pay for. To get a more elaborate effect than is required in order to sell at a given price is simply wasted effort.

Uniformity

Narrowing down the size range of yarn that you spin for sale to two or three sizes makes your yarn more interchangeable in various projects and also decreases the odds and ends of yarn you cannot readily use. When necessary, you also can grab yarn intended for one order and use it to fill a more urgent one.

In weaving with the same yarn sizes you offer for sale, your warp could be one size you sell and the weft could be the other size. This way yarn can be spun up ahead for your own weaving, but still used to fill a customer's order if necessary.

There is also an advantage to spinning more than is called for in an individual order for a specific color, because you can lay aside the extra yarn to help fill an order for assorted shades. If you can keep a backlog of a few odd colors spun up, it gives you greater variety when you need an assortment, and gets you a head start on filling the order. This is possible, of course, only if you have standardized your yarn sizes.

There is another kind of uniformity— that between all the skeins of a single order of knitting or weaving yarn. The customer

Double-woven stuffed hanging pillows, of handspun yarn. Center right has lavender glass fragments applied, with pink and purple yarn. Center left is a weed bag pillow in pinks and purples. (By Barbara L. Anderson, Urbana, Illinois)

expects, and usually wants, a certain variation within each skein to make it interesting and obviously handspun, but the *basic* yarn size must be constant. This is easier to achieve if you have limited yourself to spinning fewer different sizes of yarn for sale or for your own use. If you habitually spin only certain sizes, then it actually takes a conscious effort to deviate from them.

To check your skeins for a uniform *basic* size of yarn, measure the yarn as you wind it off into a skein, make each skein of a customer's order a predetermined number of yards, then weigh the skeins. If you are having trouble with these measured skeins not being a uniform weight (to indicate uniform basic yarn size), then spin more skeins than necessary to fill the order, and weed out the nonconforming weights. The amount of weight deviation allowable depends on the size of the yarn, for a difference of half an ounce in very heavy yarn is not noticeable, while a quarter-ounce difference in fine yarn would be too much.

Repetition

Successful selling depends on pure production, which requires endless repetition throughout the entire process. You will find you need ways to minimize the monotony.

In producing yarn, the monotony is less when you spin "assorted" shades than when you turn out three or four pounds of one color. (We find that only good music relieves the boredom of spinning one color.) Assorted skeins can be spun from layer after layer of carded wool, each layer being a different shade and consequently less boring.

In spinning two different sizes of yarn for your own use or for selling, alternating one skein of each size is not as efficient as keeping to a single size for a longer period, but it is less tedious. Using two different spinning wheels for two different sizes of yarn also makes the work physically less tiring and helps you keep each yarn to a standard predetermined size.

Earning a living from handspun usually means having something in addition to yarn, a product of some sort made from it. Repetition also can become a problem in the product itself. When producing a woven, crocheted, or knitted article that sells well, the more you do it, the more efficient you

become, but the product takes on a certain sameness. In order to maintain your own interest in what you are doing, it must present some kind of challenge other than that of just getting the work done. Only with a certain amount of risk taking can you impart real interest or excitement to the product made. However well you have planned the project in its entirety, some phase of it must be unplanned in order to have an element of surprise in it for both yourself and the customer.

For instance, I found that using an extremely variegated yarn for a simple crocheted item made it more attractive and automatically one of a kind, since using various shades of wool in the yarn gave some unexpected color combinations. The random-shaded yarn also makes it less boring for me to turn out these items, so making them is a pleasant way of keeping busy when I have spare time away from home.

To avoid the problems of repetition in our weaving, we use a "dummy" warp and a nonsystem for tying onto it. We warp up however many chains we need in whatever colors are available. Once the chains are sized and dried, we tie them on, but not as solid areas. Keeping the threads in order with the cross, we tie each chain on, scattering it across the width of the warp, and skipping over areas where that particular shade is not wanted. The chain can be tied on in a series of however many threads of this color are wanted in one place.

Then we take another chain of sized handspun and tie it on in the same manner.

Unusual handspun stuffed toys. (By Suzye Poley, Battle Creek, Michigan)

The chains overlap, but can be separated into several sections once they are tied on, and draped across chairs or other convenient objects (clear across the room if it is a long warp). This is done only to make them easier to comb out and untangle when we start rolling them onto the loom.

While it takes a little extra time to organize these overlapping chains for winding onto the loom, we have already saved that much time by making only solid color chains. It would have required changing colors too frequently if the color sequence had been planned on the warping reel.

In planning a warp that will be used for several different items, keep in mind any special requirements, such as the need to have front edges of jackets alike. We tie on both selvedge areas first, making them symmetrical for at least four inches into the warp, as these will be the front edges of our garments.

To have more latitude in putting shades where you want them without running out of colors, it helps to have more chains than are needed. On the other hand, having to make do with exactly what you have is a challenge.

You can also use handspun warps of a length to accommodate a certain number of different pieces that can be woven on the same warp and still look individual. On a forty-five-inch loom, we sometimes plan a warp for one couch throw, one coat, one vest, and two stoles (side by side). My thirty-eight-inch loom warps up for three vests, one lap robe, and four scarves or two narrow stoles.

In using "systems" like these you are designing on the loom, not on the reel, so the excitement is not over before you get to the loom.

Underproduction and Overproduction

The first year that you are selling handspun, you may not see any production-and-demand pattern emerge. You will have ups and downs, and wonder if it will ever level off to a steady flow of orders. When it does, there are two different situations that may occur.

You may have more orders than you can fill, which can be dealt with in one of two ways (or both). You can work for more speed

Knitted lace baby cap and shawl. (By Alice Stough, Millstone, West Virginia)

and efficiency, to turn out the orders faster. Or you can keep raising your prices until that slows down the flow of orders to a quantity that you can handle.

You may instead be able to spin *more* yarn than you can sell. This calls for an objective appraisal to determine the problem, which could be one or more of the following:

1. Your yarn needs more attractive packaging or labeling in order to sell better in shops or at fairs.
2. You are undersold by other spinners because your prices are too high. If you decide you cannot spin it for less, then consider taking it a step further and making a marketable article from the yarn.
3. You need to spin a more salable type of yarn. Compare it with the kinds of handspun that *are* selling. It could need to look more like handspun and less like factory-produced yarn.
4. You have not taken advantage of or been cooperative about publicity opportunities.
5. Your "customer relations" leave something to be desired. In selling wholesale, you need a certain rapport with shops, showing that you understand their marketing problems. In selling retail, you need to be responsive and helpful in dealing with individual customers.
6. You are in an area where handspun either is not a familiar commodity or too many people are spinning and competing for a limited number of

Cap of natural colored handspun two-ply, done on handmade knitting frame. (By Kay Thomas, Monaca, Pennsylvania)

customers. Try establishing markets in other parts of the country. One way would be by sending samples and wholesale price lists to shops, such as the ones that are actively seeking merchandise and are listed in each issue of *The Crafts Report* (see "Publications" in "Sources" chapter).

Deadlines

In the absence of enthusiasm, deadlines and a need for money can always be relied on. Deadlines, carefully acquired, can make production less optional. This does not mean they must be made arbitrarily, but can be made by committing yourself to specific orders at specific times.

A vital part of production is finding ways of overcoming your own inertia. Without the demands of an employer, you come to depend a great deal on initiative, the ability to do what is necessary no matter how you feel about it. Enthusiasm helps, but carries you through only certain stages, beginning when you have the whole project in your head and find it sufficiently stimulating to get you started. Then you come to a point where you have enough preliminary work done to be encouraged. Finally, you have the end in sight and it begins to look like it might work. It is the times in between that can be trying, but the astute use of deadlines can help you maintain your momentum.

Determination

It is not how easily you learn to spin that ultimately matters. It is how disciplined you are and how determined you are to sell. The intention of selling must govern how you organize everything (for example, the time you have, the work space you use) that contributes to that goal.

Good work habits can result in an astonishing amount of yarn. To get the most out of the time you have for spinning, it helps to form the habit of *steady* spinning. This is made easier if you set goals, such as a certain amount of time you must spin without stopping to rest, a certain quantity of yarn you want to spin without stopping, or a certain time of day when you will *always* spin, even if you do not feel like spinning.

Also, if the big jobs intimidate you, use the small jobs to pick up a little momentum. Once you get moving it is easier to go on than it is to stop. By the same token, any impasse can be momentarily ignored while you do some other job that is less problematic. When you get back to the original quandary, you will probably have a much clearer idea of what your options are.

Another problem is allowing yourself to be distracted by something that is unrelated to spinning and that, even though it has to be done, does not have to be done right then. When you have a task moving along nicely, try to stick with it. If you do think of something else that must be done, try to finish up the job at hand first; you will still get to the next one. Otherwise, you can get to the end of the day with quite a few things started and none completed, which can be depressing as well as unprofitable.

Flexibility

A certain adaptability or flexibility can be a hidden factor in business success. Without deadlines, it is helpful to discipline yourself to maintain regular working hours, yet when there is a deadline, normal hours will be completely disregarded. While you do not get time-and-a-half for overtime, when the emergency is over you can go fishing or something, and enjoy the fringe benefits of being your own boss.

Whatever procedure you usually follow in the processing of your wool, your plans can be disrupted by bad weather or an equipment breakdown. This should not result in no work being done, but only a change in sequence.

Flexibility in the kind of products you produce can protect you from seasonal ups and downs, and the possibility that one of your dependable outlets may change hands or go out of business. By having a variety of products, finished articles in addition to yarn, there are more kinds of outlets open to you.

In marketing, too, it is dangerous to rely completely, for instance, on one shop that will buy all you produce. Even if it appears to have a permanent management and location and is an extremely reliable customer, any catastrophe, such as a fire, could send you on a frantic search for an alternative outlet. To enjoy real freedom in self-employment, you should not be completely dependent on any one market.

Equipment

Your potential speed and efficiency in producing yarn will be partly dependent on having good equipment, and the ease with which you accomplish each process will be related to the equipment you are using. This does not mean you must start out with everything. It is better to start with the minimum, then get better tools as they become really necessary and as you decide exactly what you need. These needs will be dictated by the kind of yarn you want to produce, by your fiber source and type of fiber, and by regional problems. The spinner living close to an excellent source of custom carding, for example, is not in dire need of a carder.

Wool-Washing Tubs

Wool-washing tubs should be large enough to accommodate a sizable quantity of fleeces. We find it convenient to use double laundry tubs (from Sears, Roebuck and Company), which hold twenty gallons each and are portable, moving on casters. For twenty to thirty pounds of grease wool, fill one tub with hot water—as hot as it comes from the tap—to within four or five inches of the top. In this, dissolve ten cups of mild detergent. This may seem too much for some fleeces, but it can be too little for others, depending on how greasy they are. Since you have to add the detergent first and get it dissolved, you can note the effect the wool is having on it, and add as much wool as you feel the detergent can handle, which could be up to thirty pounds. If you put in as much fleece as the tub will contain, it is unlikely there will be too much detergent.

Once the detergent is dissolved, pull the fleeces apart and shake them as you put them into the water. Then place the cover on the tub and leave the wool to soak. When solid with wool, the water cools slowly, so you can leave it for several hours. Since it takes no longer to soak a lot of wool than it takes to soak a little, this is a good way to save time.

We remove the wash water by using a centrifugal extractor, but the "spin" cycle of a washing machine works fine if it will operate separately on "spin." If you do use a washer, confine the wool in mesh bags. (You could use old pillow cases, but mesh allows the water to spin out more efficiently.)

As the water is extracted, transfer each load to the empty half of the double laundry tub. Then replace the wash water with very warm rinse water, not too hot for your hands. The whole load of wool does not go into this at once; just take the washed wool by large double handfuls, souse it up and down, squeeze it in the rinse water, then toss it into the extractor. We use only one rinse, knowing that any remaining dirt will come out when the yarn is washed after spinning and that the finished articles we make from the yarn will also be washed. Our main purpose with the fleece washing is to eliminate all the gumminess that would interfere with smooth carding and fast spinning.

Although it is often recommended, we do not use a wire rack in the bottom of the washing tub. It is so stuffed with wool that the rack would not serve its intended purpose of allowing the dirt to settle out of the wool into the space under the rack. Much of the dirt that would have settled out, if a smaller quantity of wool were washed in the large tub, comes out instead in the rinse water, where a smaller quantity of wool is entered at a time.

Before we got the laundry tubs and the extractor, we used an old wringer washing machine with the center gyrator removed. We wrung the washed wool through the wringer, which was also used to remove the rinse water. This setup necessitated two people, one feeding the wool into the electric wringer, the other making sure the wool went on through and did not wrap itself around the rollers.

Centrifugal Extractor

The centrifugal extractor is a machine that operates like the spin cycle on a washing machine, except that it revolves much faster and therefore removes more water. This lessens the need for multiple rinsings, saves water, and cuts down on water heating costs. It is also gentle on the fleeces. When washing yarn, using the extractor is preferable to wringing out the skeins, because it puts no stress on the fibers. It also removes more water so that the yarn, like the washed fleece, dries faster. We also use it when washing and rinsing woven fabrics and blankets, taking care to remove them immediately so wrinkles do not set.

Extractors are manufactured primarily for use in industrial and coin-operated laundries and so are sturdily designed for commercial use. Suppliers are listed in the telephone directory's "Yellow Pages" under "Laundry Equipment." Used extractors sometimes are available, often because they have damaged coin boxes. The smallest model is quite adequate for wool and yarn processing.

Wringer

Using a hand wringer is the most convenient method we have found for removing excess sizing from warp chains before hanging them out to dry. A wringer can be purchased new (see "Sources" chapter) or used ones can sometimes be found in secondhand stores. An electric wringer is just as effective, but requires more attention

to prevent the chains from winding around it and getting snarled and damaged. Although a mop-bucket wringer could be used, each chain would have to be put into a mesh bag so that it could be pulled through the wringer without strain on the yarn.

Wool-Drying Racks

Drying racks can be made of any kind of rustproof wire mesh, such as chicken wire or rabbit wire. Prune-drying racks would be good, and I have seen old bedsprings used, also.

For drying large quantities of wool, you can build stackable racks with raised edges to hold them apart. These have the advantage of saving space, and also of preventing wool from blowing out of the lower racks. Shake the wool out to prevent matting while drying and also to facilitate faster drying.

Keep a plastic tarp nearby to use in case of unexpected rain. Tenting the tarp over the wool will keep off rain and let air through. In the rainy season, we use a large indoor drying rack, raising it up next to the ceiling to get the warmest air in the room.

"Cradle" Wool Picker

The picker shown and described on the following pages does a faster and more uniform teasing of wool than if it were done "by hand." In building the picker from these plans, hardwood is preferable, but high quality softwood could be used for all except the cards, which will hold the picker teeth. There may be considerable stress on these cards during the teeth-bending process, and the grain of a tough hardwood will resist splitting. This picker weighs about thirty pounds and is portable.

The top card frame picks up wool from the front bin and the teeth propel the wool from front to rear, where it drops out. You should have a box or basket there to catch the picked wool as it emerges.

Wing nuts on each end of the axis rod allow the upper card frame to be centered after assembly is completed. The upper frame must swing freely without touching either side of the base frame. The wing nuts on the eyebolts allow for the adjustment in the height of the upper card frame.

To adjust the picker for the kind of wool you are using, start with the upper card frame at a higher position than you want,

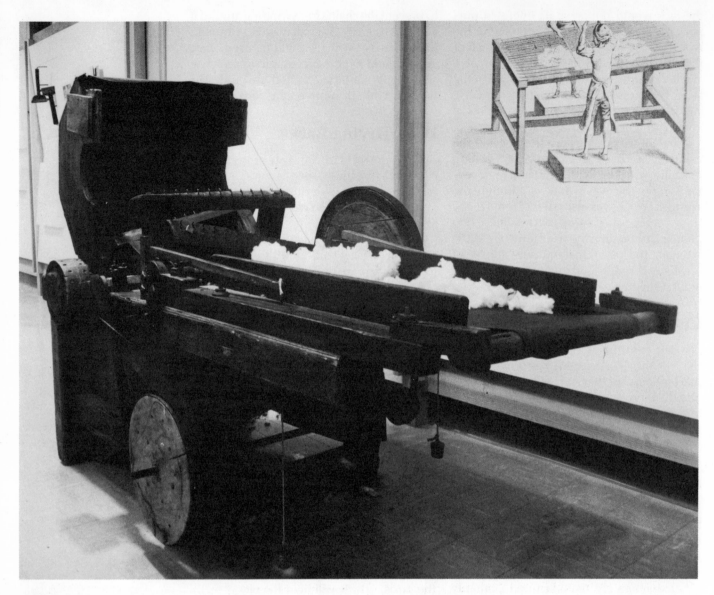

with perhaps three-eighths inch between teeth points. Gradually lower the frame until it teases well when taking small amounts of wool at a time. The farther apart you can leave the teeth, the less effort it will take to operate the picker.

This equipment is not intended to handle matted wool. If you pull the wool apart before placing it in the front bin, it will pick faster and more gently.

Be sure you are not letting it take too big a bite of wool each time. This is controlled partly by not stuffing too much wool into the bin at once. You can get more wool through it faster, and with less effort, if it catches in less at a time, allowing the frame to be swung back and forth effortlessly and rather fast. (We have timed it at about five or six minutes to pick a pound of fleece.) If the frame is not swinging easily, then it is taking too much

wool or the teeth are adjusted too close, or the wool should be pulled apart more. It will take some experimenting to get the feel of it.

More vegetation will drop out of washed fleeces in the picking than would come out of grease wool. If you do run greasy wool through the picker, it will need cleaning before using it on washed wool. Actually, there would be no reason to use it on grease wool unless the wool were going to be carded and spun in the grease.

Although much of the dirt and vegetation will fall through the cracks between the bottom cards, you will still need to brush or vacuum these cards periodically to keep the resulting teased wool cleaner. Also clean out the space below the bottom cards.

Use the picker with care, because of the sharp teeth, and keep it out of the reach of children.

Industrial wool picker from the early 1800s. This is a simply made piece of equipment and could be copied for use in a small yarn business. The wool is propelled through by the motion of the whirling picker arms, which have a uniform circumference. (Merrimack Valley Textile Museum, North Andover, Massachusetts)

Wool picker, with top card frame arm raised out of operating position to show picker teeth.

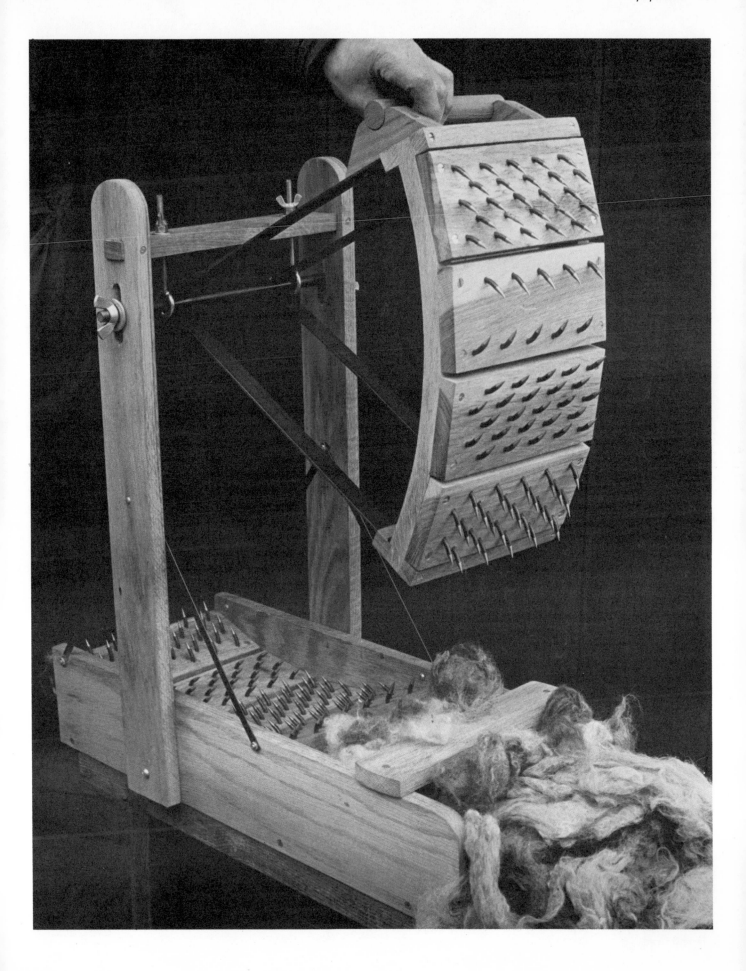

Cutting List

Begin building by laying out and cutting all the wooden pieces, except the arm handle, from about 12 board ft. of 3/4-in. stock. The rectangular hole and slot in top of the 2 arm support pieces can be made by drilling out the ends, and the middle of the waste, then finishing the sides and ends of the holes with a chisel. Drill and countersink all screw holes for #8 flathead screws.

Note: Dimensions are in inches

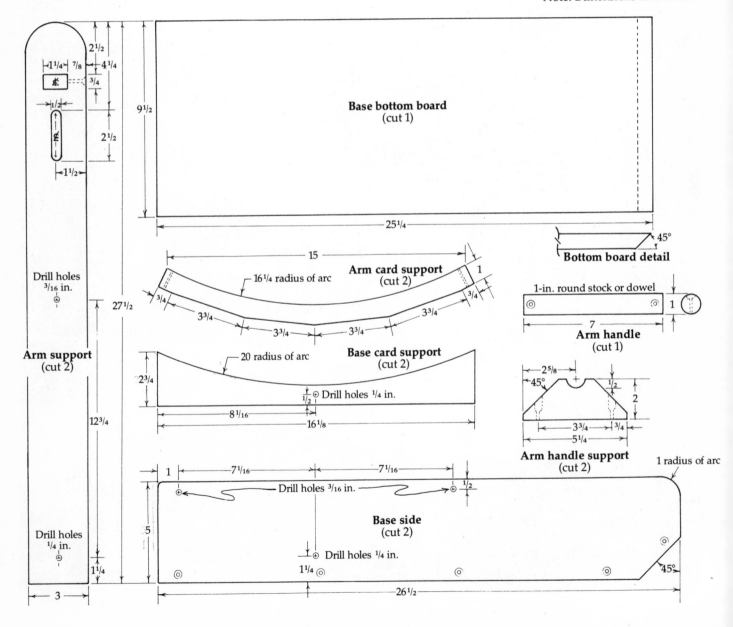

Base bottom board
(cut 1)

Bottom board detail

Arm card support
(cut 2)

16¼ radius of arc

Arm handle
(cut 1)

1-in. round stock or dowel

Base card support
(cut 2)

20 radius of arc

Drill holes ¼ in.

Arm handle support
(cut 2)

Arm support
(cut 2)

Drill holes 3/16 in.

Drill holes ¼ in.

Base side
(cut 2)

Drill holes 3/16 in.

Drill holes ¼ in.

1 radius of arc

Cutting List

Note: Dimensions are in inches

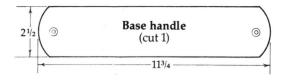

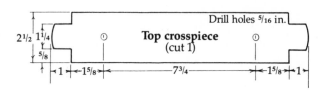

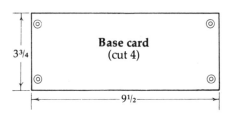

Other Hardware

Epoxy

Bright nails, 7 lb. 20 d, $^{3}/_{16}$-in. diameter

Two $^{5}/_{16}$ by 5-in. eyebolts, 4-in. stem

Two $^{5}/_{16}$-in. wing nuts with washers

Two $^{1}/_{2}$-in. wing nuts with washers, to fit axis rod

Two $^{1}/_{4}$ by 2-in. roundhead stove bolts with nuts and washers

Four $^{3}/_{16}$ by 1-in. roundhead machine screws with nuts and washers

Two $^{3}/_{16}$ by $1^{1}/_{2}$-in. roundhead machine screws with nuts and washers

Two 8-32 1-in. flathead machine screws with nuts and washers

Fifty-four #8 by $1^{1}/_{2}$-in. flathead wood screws

Two #8 by $^{3}/_{4}$-in. flathead wood screws

Sixteen $^{3}/_{4}$-in. nails

Two #8 by $^{3}/_{4}$-in. roundhead wood screws

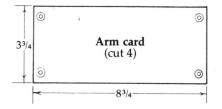

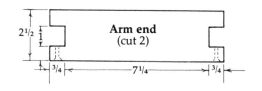

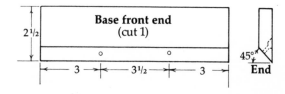

Teeth Layout

The "picker teeth"—just under 200 of them—are made from 7 lb. of 20d bright nails. Mark each nail with a file, cut to $1^3/4$-in., and sharpen to a point along about $1/2$ in. of the shank. One method of making these teeth is with a $1/2$-in. capacity drill press, a hacksaw, and 2 files (1 medium cut, 1 fine cut). Mark each nail on a jig, then chuck each one in the drill press in such a way that the jaws tighten around the shank of the nail.

Pull the nail head down to rest on the upper surfaces of the jaws, *inside* the chuck. Then tighten the chuck and turn the drill press on slow speed. The nail can be cut with the hacksaw, filed to a point, and smoothed, while revolving. If you work smoothly, you can keep the time spent shaping each tooth down to about $1^1/2$ min.

After you cut and shape the nails, lay out the teeth locations on the cards and drill with a $3/16$-in. bit. You can then start the nails into the holes, placing a drop of epoxy under each head and tapping the nails firmly in place.

When the epoxy is well cured, clamp the sides of each card in a bench vise with the teeth pointed up. Use a 6-in. (or longer) piece of $1/4$-in. iron pipe to slip over each point, and bend carefully in the proper direction. You must bend the points straight forward or backward and keep the angle and amount of bend as consistent as possible. However, in the model built for this book, the tooth lengths and heights varied by as much as $1/8$ in., yet the picker works very well.

Note: Dimensions are in inches

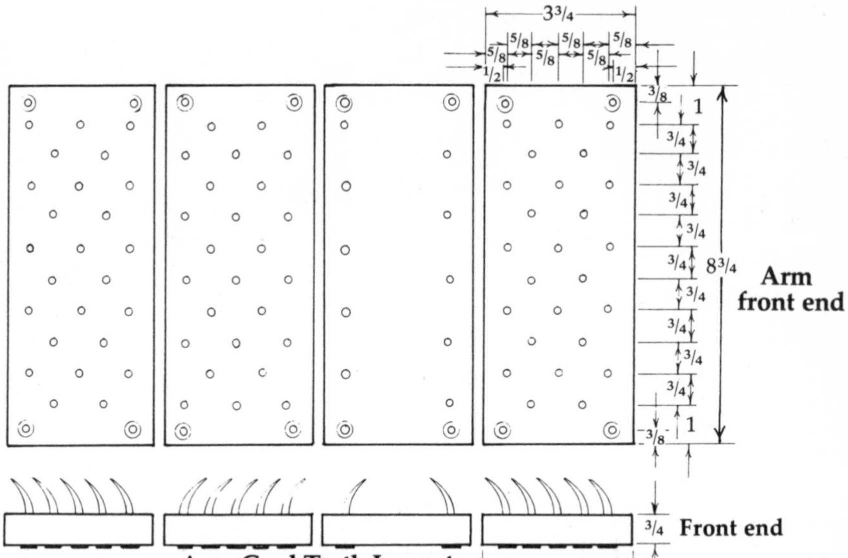

Arm Card Teeth Layout

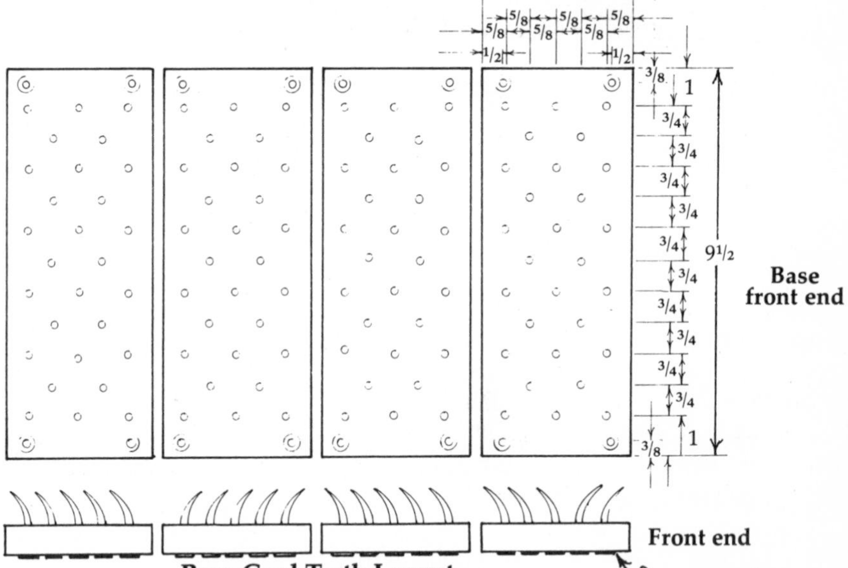

Base Card Teeth Layout

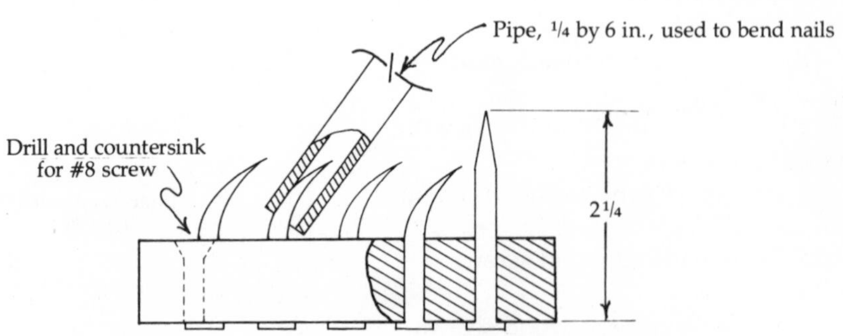

Epoxy under each nail head

Pipe, $1/4$ by 6 in., used to bend nails

Drill and countersink for #8 screw

Picker Base—Exploded Assembly Drawing

After the side pieces are screwed to the bottom board, line up the base card support pieces and clamp them in place. All 3 pieces can be drilled at once to accept 2½ by ¼-in. stove bolts. The base cards can then be screwed to the base card supports, taking care to arrange them correctly and evenly, leaving space for vegetable matter and dirt to "fall through the cracks."

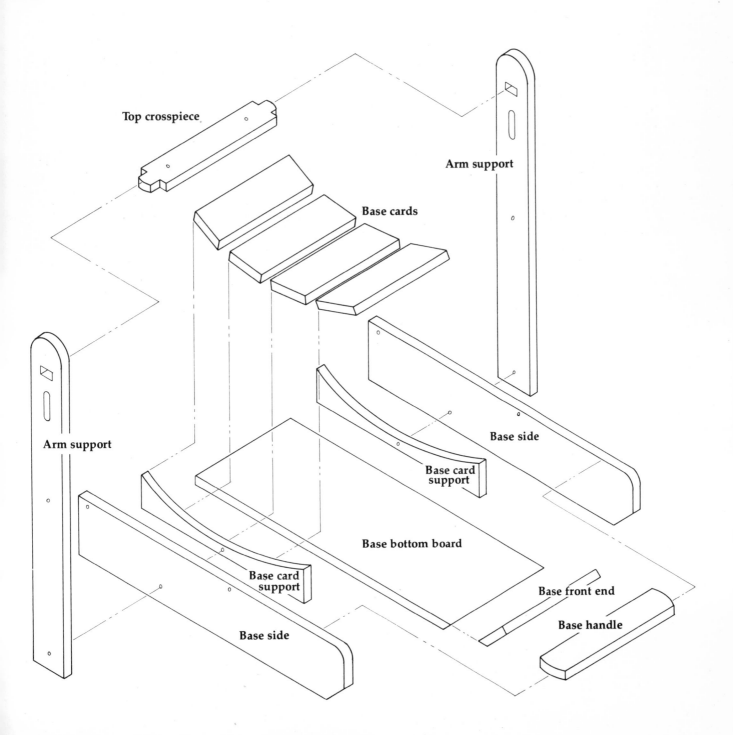

Metal Pieces

A local machine shop should have these metal sizes in stock and can cut, drill, and thread the necessary pieces. Drill the arm brackets at the ends, and bend them exactly at the center, over a ¹/₂-in. rod.

The top ends of the angle brackets can be loosely bolted to the arm supports. The bottom ends can be used to locate the ³/₁₆-in. holes in the base sides with the arm supports clamped square.

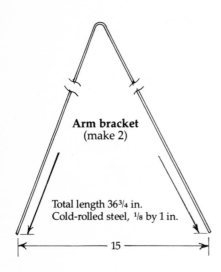

Arm bracket
(make 2)

Total length 36³/₄ in.
Cold-rolled steel, ¹/₈ by 1 in.

Note: Dimensions are in inches

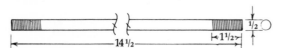

Angle bracket
(make 4)
Cold-rolled steel, ³/₄ by ³/₃₂ in.
Drill holes ³/₁₆ in.

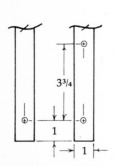

Bracket end details
Drill holes ³/₁₆ in.

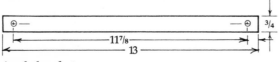

Arm support axis
(make 1)
Hot-rolled, ¹/₂-in. rod stock
Thread both ends

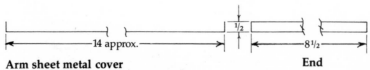

Arm sheet metal cover
(make 1)
Galvanized sheet metal 32 gauge; 15 by 8¹/₂ in.;
¹/₂-in. flange both ends

End

Picker Arm—Exploded Assembly Drawing

Bend the sheet metal arm cover by holding each end sandwiched between 2 pieces of wood and tapping with a mallet. It should fit, nailed to the concave sides of the arm card supports, tightly and squarely between the arm ends. The arm cards can be arranged and screwed to the supports without any, or with very small, cracks.

Attach the arm brackets to each end of the arm assembly. Then center the arm support axis and weld it to these brackets. Weld on the inside of the brackets to allow more adjustment room between the supporting eyebolts.

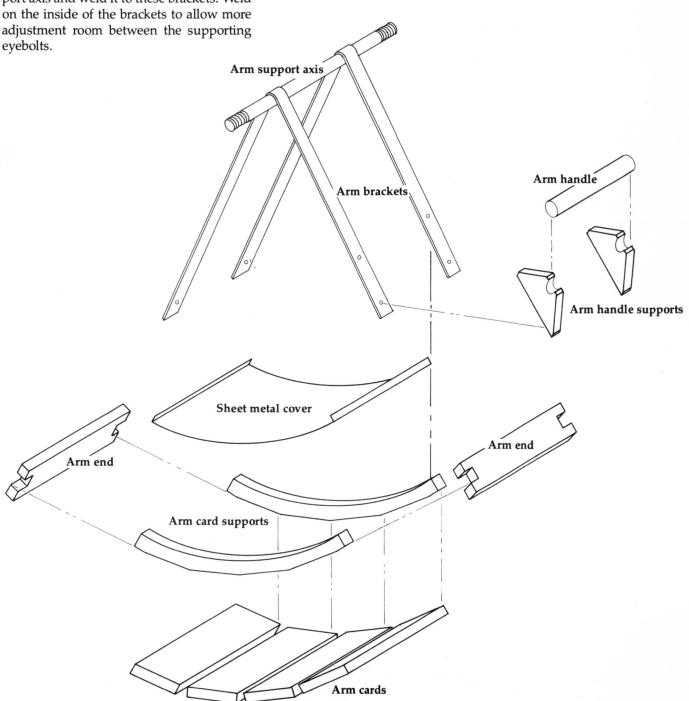

Arm support axis

Arm brackets

Arm handle

Arm handle supports

Sheet metal cover

Arm end

Arm end

Arm card supports

Arm cards

Final Assembly—Front View

Complete the final assembly, placing the eyebolts on the arm support axis and through the top crosspiece before screwing and bolting the arm supports tightly together.

Note: Dimensions are in inches

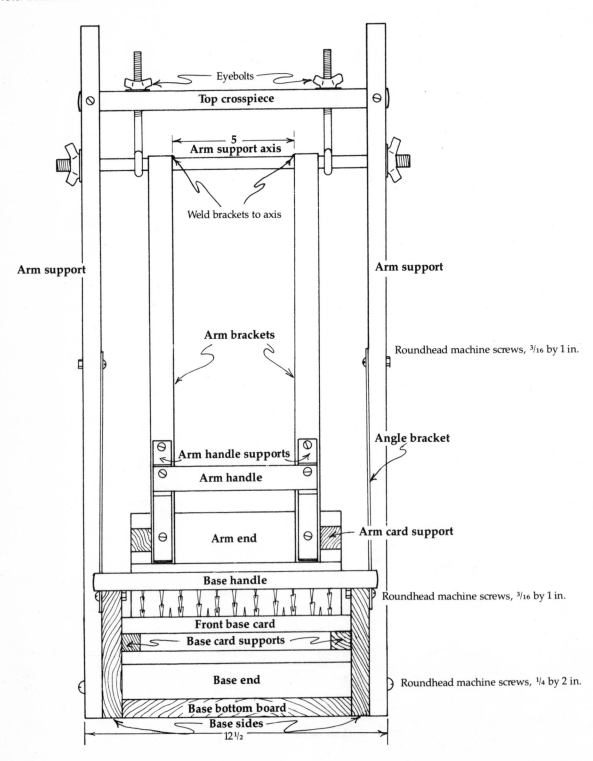

Final Assembly—Sectional Side View

Note: Dimensions are in inches

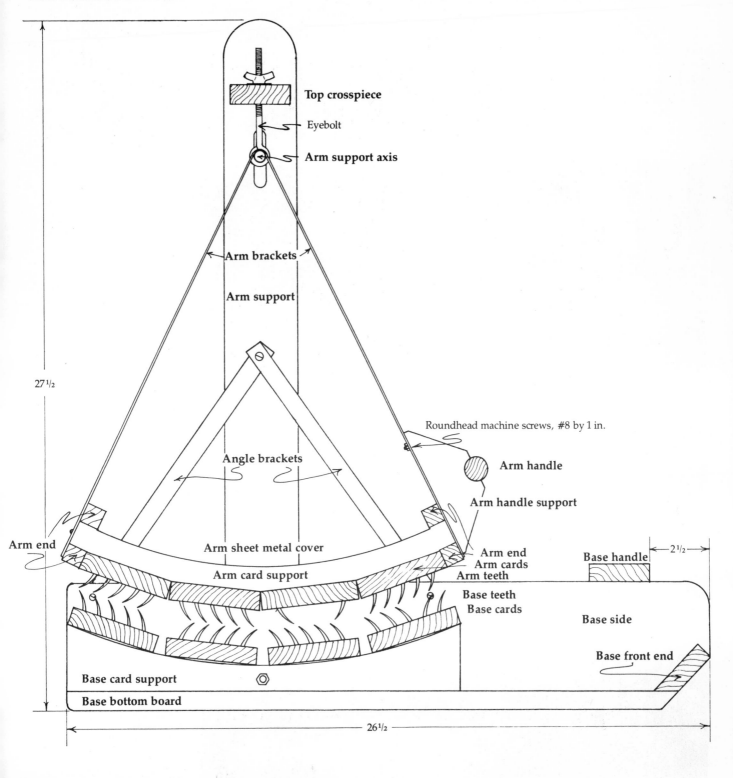

Wool Duster

A wool duster is considerably more complicated and not so necessary as the picker, but it is a useful machine if you have space for it and process a lot of wool. It is electrically powered, and can be used only on clean washed fleeces, which should previously be teased or picked to minimize fiber damage. Because of the tight hood over the revolving arms, and their tapered design with a "paddle" on each arm, the duster sucks in the wool that is placed next to the front intake. The revolving toothed arms mesh with teeth mounted inside the mechanism, picking the wool apart, while the suction and speed of the revolving arms remove small weed seeds and dust. The

Front view of duster arms, with the sheet metal hood raised.

Front view of duster used in small custom carding service. Dark opening in lower right is the wool intake. (Owner—Lorraine Wells, Portland, Oregon)

seeds drop down into a removable drawer directly under the duster arms, while the wool is blown through the outlet pipe into a wire cage. Because of the speed and force of the arms, it is most suitable for short and medium wools, and even these must be teased. (See "Sources" chapter for general plans.)

Carding or Not Carding

Some clean open fleeces can be spun into rather nice yarn without carding, and at a saving of time over hand carding. The uncarded effect is quite different, especially if you have a fleece with a lot of color variations. Other fleeces will spin up easily into a highly textured yarn, which sells well for weaving and wall hangings. Some spinners specialize in selling this heavy rough yarn made from uncarded wool. One friend of mine refers to it (privately) as her "garbage yarn" and has trouble keeping up with the orders.

For fleeces needing a very minimum of carding, the flick carder may do just the amount of fluffing up that is necessary.

Drum Carders

Hand-operated drum carders can be purchased, or built at home. (Plans for building a drum carder, and a list of sources of card clothing, can be found in *Spinning and Weaving with Wool*.) Some makes give the option of several interchangeable drums

with different carding teeth, which is an idea you can use if you are making your own. You can make home-built carders larger if desired—either wider, or even a narrower width and a larger diameter to produce a long strip of carded wool. You can also motorize a drum carder to free your hands for teasing and feeding in the fleece. The motor speed should be geared down to not much faster than if turned by hand—about sixty to seventy revolutions per minute.

Wool should be well teased before carding. A motorized drum carder with a chain and sprocket will have a more positive drive, but a belt that allows slippage is less likely to damage the wool or the card clothing, if it gets stalled by snarls in the wool.

Drum carder made wider and larger than standard drum carder, but still turned by hand. (Owner–Sophia Block, West Tisbury, Massachusetts)

Home-built motorized carder with one-sixth horsepower gear motor, which turns at 90 revolutions per minute, but wheels are such that the effective rpm is 67½. (Owner–Dorothy Eckmann, Savannah, Georgia)

Custom Carding

Some mills (see "Sources" chapter) will do custom carding of wool for handspinners. Nearly all of these mills require washed fleeces. Unless you are sending to a mill in your own part of the country, postage charges on top of the fees charged for carding can make it quite expensive.

The disadvantages of mill carding are that the machinery is so large that it tends to overcard, eliminating any subtlety in shading and texture, and causes considerable breakage of longer fibers. Also, a small amount of the wool is lost in the carding machine.

Some large mills are unable to card small amounts of wool and return that same wool to you; you will get back the same amount you sent, but your own wool will have been carded with other orders.

With most small mills, however, you are able to get your own wool back, even in quantities of as little as five or ten pounds. This is important if you are sending dark wool. Keep in mind, though, that these mills will card only washed fleeces. If you send several bags with different shades, plainly mark them to be carded separately. While the machine carding results in solid colors—without the variations that you can get with a drum carder—you can send several separate shades for carding, then when you are ready to spin, you can take thin layers from each of the batts and spin them up together. The result can be a subtly variegated yarn with a

Carding machine that was custom-built in England in the style of the first American-built carding machine (of about 1804), which was water powered and had one more set of worker-stripper rollers. (Owners—Ross and Paula Simmons)

hand carded look.

Beautiful fleeces are best done at home, but some wools will be more usable after mill carding. Some spinners wash and set aside all the tags and belly wool, odds and ends of semimatted fleeces, and any wool that is too much of a chore to card by hand. When there is enough to sort into ten pounds or more of light, medium, and dark, they bag it up and send it to the nearest carding mill.

Fleeces must be washed completely grease-free if they are to be custom carded. Most of the carding places (see "Sources" chapter) will reject wool that is even slightly "sticky," because if this were carded, it would cause a grease buildup on their equipment. From the standpoint of the spinner, the machine carding of "sticky wool" is undesirable as the fibers do not slip past each other freely and therefore suffer a considerable amount of unnecessary damage.

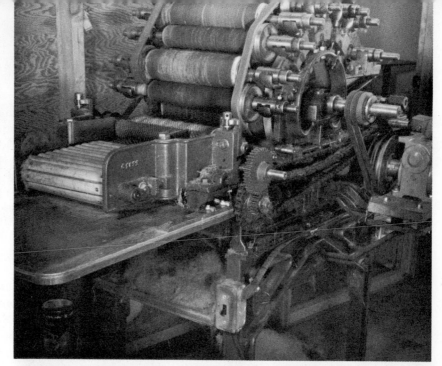

Yarn Blocker

In addition to removing any remaining dirt, the purpose of washing yarn after it is spun is to preshrink it, relax the fibers, and set the twist. The best way to set the twist is to dry the yarn with moderate tension on *all* the yarn in the skein. This is not effectively accomplished by hanging skeins with a weight, because every inch of the yarn is not evenly weighted. Yarn wound onto a blocker, however, dries under even tension.

Before using a blocker, wash and rinse the yarn, then remove water from the skein by wringing it out, or by using an extractor or the "spin" cycle of a washing machine. Then put the skein on a swift, one end of the skein fastened to a blocker stave, and wind the yarn from the swift onto the blocker, guiding the yarn so it forms a neat skein on the blocker. Loop and tie each end of the yarn back around the skein before adding another skein to the blocker. Leave the yarn there until it is dry.

Yarn thus dried will be easier to use in knitting than yarn not dried on a blocker because it will have less tendency to curl or kink while you knit. The blocking cannot remove overtwist, but it does minimize it. Blocked yarn is also more reliable to use in weaving either warp or weft as all parts of the skein react the same, resulting in better selvedges. In tapestry weaving, the weft yarn does not pull in the edges as much and

does not pull in unevenly, which is especially important.

For plain yarns, the blocker greatly improves the appearance of the skein, but some specialty yarns may best be left unblocked. One yarn type that should not be blocked is a thick-and-thin blobby yarn, in which you want to enhance the fluffiness of the slub.

The reel of the standard blocker (see "Sources" chapter for information about getting blocker plans) is about twenty-four inches long and about one and one-half yards in diameter. It can hold from two to ten skeins of yarn, depending on the bulk of each skein and how much you want to spread them out to facilitate faster drying. The reel lifts out of the base, so you can move the reel to the warmest place in the house or

Mill sample carder used in small custom carding business. Some parts of this have been rebuilt so it can handle longer, coarser wools, which some sample carders cannot do. (Owner–Lorraine Wells, Portland, Oregon)

This standard sized yarn blocker can be made from plans (see "Sources" chapter).

"Giant" blocker, mainly used outdoors in the summer, catches overflow from standard blockers. In addition to the space it takes up, it also has the disadvantage of making skeins a little too large for easy use. (Owners—Ross and Paula Simmons)

outside on a warm or breezy day. As soon as the skeins are dry, slip them off the blocker.

This is a simple and inexpensive piece of equipment to build and need not be stained or varnished. It should not have a finish that will be damaged by damp yarn wound on it. You can make it out of used lumber, and the only smooth surfaces needed are the edge of the reel staves (where the yarn touches it) and the handle used to turn it. For drying larger quantities of yarn at one time, you can make several reels to fit onto the same base.

A horizontal warping reel could be used for the same purpose, except that without a handle it is not easy to turn it as fast as you can turn the blocker, and the resulting skeins are too large for convenience.

On the other hand, the blocker plans can be modified for use as a warping reel for short warps, such as one-of-a-kind items. Simply build the end supports about four inches higher. Make holes to position removable dowels, for making the cross in your warp, along the edge of one end of the reel. It will also need a hole in each of the staves, at the opposite end, for optional placement of the dowel used for the other end of the warp chain.

If you are doing only one skein of warp yarn a day, that skein could be washed and wound onto the blocker in the form of a warp chain, and left to dry before chaining it off (and sizing it later). Before removing the chain, be sure to secure the cross by tying.

To see how much difference it makes to block a skein of yarn instead of hanging it to dry, wind a damp skein around the back of a kitchen chair (one that will not be damaged by the dampness) and leave it there until it is dry.

Spinning Wheels

An extensive selection of available treadle spinning wheels is shown in *Spinning and Weaving With Wool*. In choosing a spinning wheel for production use, consider the following:

1. You may need more than one wheel if you are spinning several very different types of yarns. An all-purpose wheel is seldom ideally suited for the outer limits of both fine and heavy yarn.
2. Get a *drive ratio* that is fast enough for the size yarn you will be spinning. Fast spinning of fine yarn requires a much higher drive ratio than that needed for medium yarn. The larger the drive wheel, the higher the potential speed can be, given the necessary pulley sizes. (The smaller the pulley in relation to the drive wheel, the higher and faster the drive ratio.) The drive ratio of double belt wheels can be changed, within certain limits, by having several bobbins with different pulley diameters. The drive ratio of single belt wheels can also be changed by having an assortment of extra whorls.
3. Be sure the *pulley ratio*, on a double belt wheel, is adequate to draw in the

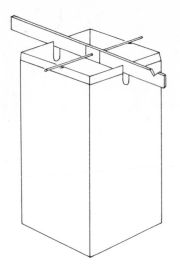

size yarn you will be spinning. The larger the flyer pulley in relation to the bobbin pulley, the greater the speed and force by which the yarn is drawn onto the bobbin. The degree of force is important in spinning medium and heavy yarns. The best solution is to have several flyer whorls, thus allowing a variety of ratios from which you can choose.

4. Be sure the flyer and bobbin are well balanced. If in doubt, ask—and get the answer in writing. Then if the balance is faulty, you will be justified in sending back the flyer assembly and requesting one that is balanced. This is especially important for a fast wheel, and even for a slower wheel that will be used for production spinning of medium yarns. If a flyer

The McMorran Yarn Balance provides a simple way to figure the number of yards per pound of any yarn—by weighing a small snip. Available from Grandor Industries (see "Sources" chapter).

A number of these automatic electric spinners were built about 1950 for the National Industries for the Blind, which later closed out their spinning project. We bought one machine; the rest went into storage and have since been sold. It is more suitable for fine yarn than for heavy yarn. (Owners—Ross and Paula Simmons)

assembly is out of balance, it will be noisy and will wear out faster.

5. Get bobbins that have bearings in each end. They last longer and are less noisy than a loose-fitting bobbin without bearings. A close-fitting bobbin without bearings has the full length of the bobbin core rubbing against the spindle, which creates a noticeable surface friction and is especially troublesome when winding off fine yarn. My own experience has been that a bobbin without bearings will not respond quickly—really snapping in the yarn—which is important for fast spinning. Since almost half of your spinning time is spent waiting while the yarn draws onto the bobbin, the slightest hint of sluggishness can be annoying.

6. Check the size of the bobbin, which determines the yarn capacity. Most spinners feel that a bobbin length of three and one-half or four inches is adequate for only fine yarn, with a five- to seven-inch length more suitable for medium-sized yarns. Many wheels that are otherwise well designed for medium yarn are found to have bobbins that are frustratingly short. "Bulk spinners" for spinning heavy yarn are nearly all made eight to ten inches long and are well suited for their purpose.

7. Have some understanding about the purchase of spare parts or the replacement of parts that wear out too

Front and side views of Japanese electric spinner. Three speeds—2200, 1400, and 900 revolutions per minute; sliding yarn guide; orifice five millimeters (just less than one-fourth inch); reverse switch. All correspondence must be in Japanese. Available from Nakui Seisakusho (see "Sources" chapter).

Kircher Spinning Machine. Electric semiautomatic, with yarn position lever; orifice one-half inch; bobbin length five inches; 5000 revolutions per minute. Available from Firma Kircher or Greentree Ranch (see "Sources" chapter).

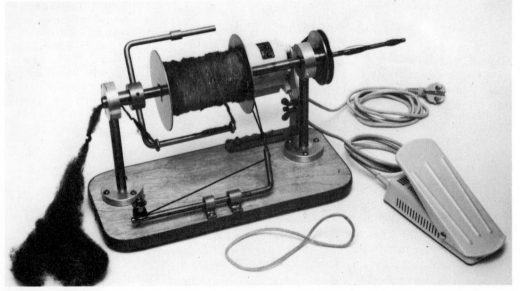

Speedy Spinner. Electric semi-automatic, with yarn position lever; orifice 7.5 millimeters (a little over ¼ inch); bobbin length 100 millimeters (4 inches); motor speed 2000 revolutions per minute, but drive of cylinder is not that fast. Available from Plix Products (see "Sources" chapter).

soon. Be sure the maker understands that your spinning wheel will be used for production work. Your own cooperation is needed to clean and oil the parts that need oiling.

Electric, Automatic, and Semiautomatic Spinners

Electric and semiautomatic or automatic spinners are presented here because they have the potential for speed (although all are not super fast) and because they have not been fully covered in other books. (As I have not tried all the wheels pictured here, I cannot vouch for how well each of them performs.) A motorized spinner may or may not be more efficient than a treadle wheel, de-pending on such factors as yarn size and texture and how the fibers are carded.

Electric spinners are ordinarily more portable than treadle wheels, but cannot be taken beyond the range of electric power. They take less physical effort for long hours of spinning, and can be used by persons who suffer some disability in their legs. With the exception of the motorized bulk-spinner head, most electric spinners are best suited to the spinning of finer weights of yarn.

Automatic winding spinners are clearly of advantage in the time saved over chang-ing yarn from hook to hook, or stopping to move a sliding yarn guide on the flyer. This feature saves time on a treadle wheel just as it does on an electric one. Semiautomatic spinners allow you, without stopping spinning, to change the place where the yarn winds onto the spool by moving a spool-position arm or lever by hand.

While the physical strain may be lessened by using an electric wheel, a kind of nervous fatigue can result from spending long hours with a machine. Some electric spinners make an almost unbearable amount of noise.

In shopping for an electric spinner, you will need to ask the manufacturer some questions, unless you are able to try out the machine before buying it. Some information, such as orifice size, bobbin length, and pulley ratio, is usually provided. I would suggest you also ask the following questions:

1. Does it have a balanced flyer?
2. Are the motor or other moving parts unusually noisy?
3. What is the efficient maximum flyer speed, if it is different from the stated speed of the motor?
4. Is there excessive vibration?
5. Does it need to be fastened down during use?
6. Does it have bearings in the bobbin?
7. If it is foreign made, does it work when plugged into our electric outlets?
8. Is there a guarantee on the motor?
9. Will the manufacturer replace parts if they wear out within a certain time?
10. Is it suitable for high-speed use, or for production use for long periods of time?

Spinskeiner. Treadle automatic; spun yarn wound automatically into a skein; orifice one-half inch; drive ratio to order. Patent pending. Available from Felix Stephens (see "Sources" chapter).

Electric bulk spinner; orifice one inch. This can be easily made by motorizing a bulk spinner head, or see "Sources" chapter for manufacturers.

Treadle automatic; orifice three-eighths inch (larger to order); bobbin four inches (larger to order). Available from Bud Kronenberg (see "Sources" chapter).

Business Matters

Just about the first thing you should do when you start selling yarn, or even when you start *intending* to sell, is to get yourself set up as a "business." It is necessary to establish the fact, as soon as possible, that you *qualify* as a business so that you can legitimately deduct all your early expenses, which are usually quite heavy. The cost of your spinning wheel, carder, business stationery, advertising, and travel to fairs, as well as the cost of buying your fleeces (or of raising sheep) and a portion of your home working area expenses are all business deductions if you sell yarn. Keep detailed records of all these expenses, and also record your spinning income carefully, expecting it to be outweighed by expenses at first. If you or your spouse is working part time or full time, the losses in your spinning business may bring some refund of the withholding taxes paid, since income tax is concerned with your *total* income. That first year, it is unlikely you will be showing a profit above your entire expenses. Because of this, you need to make it clear that your spinning is a business and not a hobby, so that the deduction of any loss cannot be "disallowed." The way the rules are now, the Internal Revenue Service allows several years of business losses if you can prove you are trying to operate a profitable business. Although the time limit is subject to change, you now must show a profit in two years out of five. After several years of profit, you might still go "in the red" if you build a new studio or sheep barn or have some other unusually large expense.

Establishing Your Business

Handling your business in a business-like manner from the beginning is going to be of advantage in a number of ways, not the least of which is showing the seriousness of your intentions if you are questioned by the Internal Revenue Service.

In any state that has a retail sales tax, you legally are required to obtain a tax number and collect sales tax on all retail sales. This number not only says you are in business, but also entitles you to *buy* wholesale. However, on anything you purchase wholesale for your personal use (in other words, anything that does not go into the making of yarn or other items you will be selling) or any purchased supplies that are for use in your business but are not going into an article for resale, you still will either have to pay sales tax to the wholesaler or pay a "use tax" on it. In most states, the sales tax return has a place to declare this use tax.

If you are in a city or an incorporated town, look into getting a business license. Some towns have special permits for what they call "home occupations." Even if your home is in a residential area not zoned for business, you can still do mail-order selling. Home craft businesses usually can be conducted by mail from any location, without a license.

Having printed stationery that has your logo and business address on it looks more businesslike, both to the IRS and your customers. This could be offset printed quite inexpensively. If your address is temporary, you could get a post office box, so that the address remains permanent despite any change of residence. Also, having a box number is safer than having a street address when you are expecting checks in the mail.

Keep accurate, detailed records of all the money you earn as well as all expenses, including mileage and the reason for each trip. Save both receipts and canceled checks to substantiate your expenses. For the small items I buy for business use, such as tape, envelopes, index cards, and pens, I save their labels as "positive proof of purchase"; these things otherwise would not be identified either on a sales slip or on a check.

Also keep a record of business-related correspondence and phone calls. This is a bit of paper work to store, but for the first few years, these letters and records will help establish the fact that you are conscientiously trying to make a profit. For example, if you send out a mailing of price lists and samples to shops in order to stimulate wholesale orders, keep track of the shops as well as all the expenses involved. You should do this for your own information, but also to substantiate the seriousness of your intentions.

If there is a guild of professional craftsmen in your area, consider joining. Your dues are business deductible, and your membership could enhance your professional standing as well as your opportunities.

Separate Checking Account

When establishing a craft business, having a separate checking account for business is frequently recommended. But with a separate account, you must keep *unusually* detailed records of all transactions involving *both* accounts, in case you have to explain them to the Internal Revenue Service. The first step in an audit is to check your total bank deposits against the income you reported.

During the time when yarn sales are not sufficient to pay all business-related bills, you will be feeding personal money into your business account. While this is to be expected, it causes a potential tax difficulty. By depositing personal checks into your business account, you will in effect be putting more into it than you report as business income.

Even after you reach a point where your

business checking account does not need subsidizing by personal funds, money transferred back and forth can still result in the same sum being deposited twice. It can happen like this: You are at the grocery store with the wrong checkbook, so you pay your bill with a business check of twenty dollars. Then, when you get home, you write a check from your personal account to repay the borrowed money. That twenty dollars has now been deposited twice. Or, you may have a large personal bill to pay and not quite enough money in your personal account, so you write a check from your business account, knowing you can soon pay it back with personal income. When you return this money, you again make a double deposit. Unless you keep very detailed records in both your business and personal bank accounts, you will have trouble explaining the situation.

If you open a retail shop, it is hard to get by without having a separate checking account, but for a home-studio business or a mail-order business, it may prove simpler to handle everything out of the same account, which is what we do. However, even with one checking account, we still can have problems. We deposit all the money we earn into it, then when we have an excess in the checking account, we write a check and deposit it into our savings. This is a good idea, because the money earns interest. But if we need more money back in the checking account in order to pay large business expenses, we transfer it from savings into checking. Adding up these redeposits totals more money than we made, as some of it is added twice or three times. Without the canceled checks and a record of all these transactions, we would have an explanation of the discrepancies, but would have no way of proving it.

Estimated Tax

When a person is self-employed or has an income from which no withholding taxes are taken, the Internal Revenue Service requires the filing of an Estimated Tax Declaration (Form 1040 ES) and payment quarterly, in advance, on the estimated income. (The form itself is comparatively simple.) While it is difficult for a craftsman to make an accurate estimate of income for the next year, you can amend the estimate from quarter to quarter if it appears your income will be more or less than originally calculated. The nearest IRS office can help you with any difficulties, and has a bulletin to explain this tax.

If in the beginning you or your spouse is working at a salaried job, you may be able to postpone the income estimating for a while by having enough *extra* withholding taxes deducted to cover the amount of income made from spinning. While the IRS does not encourage this, they tolerate it because your taxes are still computed on the basis of your *total* income. Once your business is well established and your annual income levels off, the estimating of income will not be so problematic. And you ordinarily can stay within the law just by estimating the same income this year that you had last year, then adjusting it upward or downward as necessary at the end of the year. If you pay to have your taxes prepared, this will be set up for a whole year, and you just have to send in the predetermined amount quarterly, and let the accountant refigure it at the beginning of the next year. At that time, you will either owe more tax or have a credit toward the following year.

Tax Accountants

In the beginning, we found it advantageous to have an accountant do our taxes and set us up with a simple system of recording income and expenses. Professional tax consultants are well informed about the full range of legal deductions, the business expenses that can be counted as legitimate expenses, and the changes that occur in the tax rules. They can tell you, for instance, what expenses can be spread out by depreciation and, on large purchases, which of the two depreciation formulas should be used. They also will know how to charge for your auto use. Ordinarily, when your yarn selling is only a minor portion of your income, an accountant may advise that it is impractical to deduct a percentage of your auto expenses and may recommend that you keep a record of the mileage that is related to your spinning income. This can be deducted at a flat rate per mile (the rate varies each year) from your taxes.

You might ask other craftsmen about accountants who prepare their taxes in order to find someone who is particularly knowl-

This form can be either an invoice to bill a customer or an order for supplies, and also serves as advertising.

Spinning Wheels
Looms
Drop Spindle
Carders
Books

The River Farm

ROUTE 1, BOX 169A
TIMBERVILLE, VA 22853
(703) 896-9931

Fleece
Homespun Yarn
Black Sheep
Weaving &
Spinning Lessons

SHIP TO _____

_____

_____

DATE_____

INVOICE NO. _____

ORDER NO. _____

QUANTITY	DESCRIPTION	PRICE

CPP 2206

edgeable about tax rulings relevant to craft income. Also, you would have some assurance that such accountants would take what you do seriously and try to save you money.

After a few years of having professional help, you will have a clear idea of how taxes are done, and may decide to do your own, patterned after the returns of previous years. The Internal Revenue Service puts out free information booklets, one of which is especially helpful—*Tax Guide for Small Businesses*. Good pamphlets also are available free from the Small Business Administration, P.O. Box 15434, Fort Worth, Texas 76119; and for a small fee from the Superintendent of Documents, Government Printing Office, Washington, D.C. 20402.

Sales Tax Reports

Do not pay anyone to do your retail sales tax return, because no one could save you any money. You owe an exact sum, determined by the income you made from retail sales, and there is only one way to determine it correctly. If the form looks too complicated the first time, the state tax people can be helpful, either on the phone or at their office, and will not charge you for their assistance. After you have done it once, the next time it will be easy.

In a state that has a sales tax, you collect it only on the retail sales made within the state. However, most states require your sales tax report to list *all* sales, whether retail or wholesale, in-state or out-of-state. You do not have to collect tax or pay tax to the state on the amount of your retail sales that are out-of-state. You also do not have to collect or pay on any of the wholesale, although it must be separated as in-state or out-of-state on the report. So the important things to record, on all money you take in, is whether it is retail or wholesale and whether it was sold within the state or not. The easiest way to do this is to make out a separate sales slip for each transaction, so that the slips can be sorted out into the four separate categories at the end of each tax period.

Bookkeeping

Careful record keeping is a legal necessity and also an advantage. Having an exact tabulation of your expenses allows you to deduct them from your income and not pay taxes on the amount that was not profit. Your records also will help you know how much actual spinning income would be necessary to get past the stage where money is only changing hands and into the stage where you are making money beyond your total expenses. And records give you a basis for deciding what part of your spinning activity is making money and what part is not.

Develop a system for keeping track of all expenses and for recording all income. Your system does not have to be elaborate—it just needs to be consistent. Spending too much time on accounting subtracts from the time you could be spending in production. But only with accurate bookkeeping can you take full advantage of any and all tax breaks, and those tax breaks can make the difference between profit and loss.

To be able to find needed information easily, I record it on a separate large piece of paper for each month, entering daily a detailed notation of expenses. A *daily* log of money matters keeps anything from being forgotten. Receipts for each month are kept in a separate long envelope. At the end of each month I transfer the expense figures from the monthly page onto my ledger, then file away the monthly list and the corresponding receipts in a large manila envelope.

Make it a habit to ask for a receipt for every purchase, no matter how small, and put it away in the "month-envelope" when you get home. If you request it, postal clerks will give you a receipt stamped with a postmark when you buy stamps. In a mail-order business, postal expenses could seem so high in relation to your income that the Internal Revenue Service might challenge them. Postmarked receipts prove that the purchases in question were made, and when.

A large "accordian" file envelope will hold your accumulation of records for that year. After referring to it to figure your taxes, put a copy of the year's tax return and all your canceled checks in it, then mark it with the year on the outside and store it. Keep the whole file on hand for at least seven years.

Deductions for Home-Studio

The rulings concerning use of your home for business purposes recently have become more strict. Now for expenses to be deductible, your home must be the *primary* place of business. This could mean that if you have a retail shop, your home expenses for the part of your house that you use for spinning or storage may not be allowed as a deduction unless you prove real necessity for its use.

The key words concerning home business use are *"regular* and *exclusive* use of the *space"* for business purposes. "Space" is now defined as a room or rooms. (A preferable definition would be "a partitioned area.") This means that you should concentrate your spinning equipment and supplies in a single room or several rooms so that the entire space is used for business items.

It can make quite a difference if you *are* able legally to deduct part of your home expenses. For instance, if you have five rooms and use two exclusively for carding, spinning and/or weaving, then close to two fifths of your rent or property tax, your utilities, insurance, repairs, and so on could add up to an appreciable amount. It can also be calculated as the exact percentage of the square feet of the rooms you use for business in relation to the whole house (not including the bathroom).

Some craftsmen have been quite concerned that this "regular and exclusive use of *space"* eventually could be more narrowly interpreted as "a separate structure," which in many instances is not a practical arrangement.

However, if your studio-shop is in a separate building adjoining your home, it is completely deductible.

Social Security Taxes

If your net earnings for the year are over four hundred dollars, then you must file and pay self-employment tax (Schedule 1040 SE). There are quite a few lines to fill in, but what it amounts to is multiplying your net profit by .081, or whatever rate is given each year on the form, to determine the tax.

The self-employed person really pays somewhat more taxes for social security coverage than someone does who is paid a salary. The salaried person has an employer who also contributes a portion of the total amount of the individual's social security tax. The craftsman, being her own employer, must pay the entire amount, which is more than what a salaried employee would pay on the same income. While there are many advantages to being self-employed, this tax arrangement is not one of them.

Keogh Plan

The Keogh Plan is a method whereby a self-employed person can set aside money in a private "retirement fund." The advantage is that you can defer income tax payment on this money until it is withdrawn during retirement. The plan is recommended with the general assumption that when you retire your income will be considerably less, putting you in a lower tax bracket than at the time you were depositing the funds. If so, this should result in less income tax being paid on the Keogh Plan money when it is drawn out, after your retirement. The amount you can put in is determined as a percentage of your net self-employment income (up to fifteen percent, ordinarily). Any bank can give you a pamphlet on the current regulations, and will not charge to advise you on how much of an actual advantage it would be to you, given your amount of income and your age. The Internal Revenue Service also has printed information about it.

Because of the annual fee charged by the bank or institution that is trustee of the funds, and because your money is tied up out of reach (unless you become disabled) until after you reach age fifty-nine and one-half, you will want to weigh the advantages against the disadvantages. You will still have to pay income tax on the money (and on the interest it earned) when it is withdrawn. And when working at home, without the hardship of commuting to a job, there is not the same incentive for retirement, to "get out of the rat race." So, if you do not retire, you may not necessarily *be* in a lower income bracket. With this in mind, you might choose to invest in high-interest, long-term savings certificates, with the income tax already paid on the money, and have these for your retirement.

On the other hand, the Keogh Plan has one special advantage in the first few years of selling, when your income could be so small that you might not have the $1,000 minimum deposit required to purchase a savings certificate (certificate of deposit). The Keogh Plan has no minimum deposit condition, and most savings and loan banks pay interest on Keogh funds at the same rate as they pay on eight- to ten-year certificates. It also has the advantage of forcing you to keep your money in savings, once you deposit it, so that you *do* have money saved up for retirement.

Insurance

The types of insurance you would want if you have a retail shop are different from what you need if you have a mail-order business, or even a studio-shop that is open only by appointment.

Fire insurance is something you ordinarily would have on your residence. In some instances it can be expanded to include your equipment and supplies, if you have a small mail-order business in yarn selling. From a business angle, fire insurance is more urgent when you have quite a bit of expensive equipment and could be put out of business by a home fire. In the case of a retail shop, the *building* is customarily insured by the owner, the *contents* by the party who is renting or leasing. You usually do not insure what you do not own, unless this insurance is required by the terms of your rental or lease agreement.

Liability insurance is for your own protection in case a customer is injured on your premises. When your home does not contain an actual shop that is open during specific hours, with people regularly coming and going, a homeowner's policy can sometimes be amended to specifically cover customers. The cost of a liability policy inclusive of both home and home-business would be partially a business expense. On the other hand, a policy that is specifically for the benefit of your business would be entirely a business expense.

Normally, a policy to cover theft of merchandise is worth considering only if you keep a lot of made-up merchandise on hand, or consign a large quantity of goods to shops and galleries that are not insured, or send to many uninsured exhibits. The policy should be worded especially to include merchandise that is out on consignment, as this is an area of high risk. However, the reason many shops do not have theft insurance is because it is expensive; this cost also makes it impractical for most craftsmen to have their own.

Pricing

It is difficult to have a clear idea of what something is worth when there is not just a simple time factor involved. Yet a fair and firm price is crucial to your whole operation, and must precede any selling. And even though you anticipate only retail sales, you must also give some thought to the eventuality of wholesaling, so that it will have a place in your price structure. Since buyers for craft shops frequently look through craft fairs for things to sell in their own shop, it helps to be fully prepared—to be able to give an exact answer to an exact question.

Pricing Theory

There are two general ways of determining prices for crafts, and they would appear to apply to handspun yarn and also to weaving. *Backward pricing* means you start by determining the realistic retail price you think could be charged in the marketplace—either in retail shops or galleries or at fairs, or direct to the retail customer by mail. From that established retail price, you work *backward* to establish a consignment and/or wholesale price. Ordinarily, a consignment price would be around sixty percent of the retail price, meaning that the shop takes forty percent. And when selling actual wholesale, direct to a retail shop that is purchasing your yarn or other items outright, you usually get one half of the retail price. What they buy for fifty cents, they sell for a dollar. With yarn, where you have competition from both imported handspun and from other spinners in this country, backward

pricing may be the way you have to go.

Forward pricing starts out by totaling the cost of materials, adding to it what you consider a reasonable wage per hour, plus overhead and other indirect or hidden expenses, plus a profit. This total represents what you would like to have as your *wholesale* price, the smallest amount you would accept. Doubling this amount will give you your retail price, and forty percent less than retail will be the consignment price.

If you feel you cannot afford to allow a wholesale or consignment discount, then you will have to rely on selling directly to the customer by mail, or in your own studio-shop, or in craft fairs, which take a moderate commission.

If you have an unusual item, with nothing too much like it on the market, the forward pricing may be practical. With anything woven, knitted, or otherwise made from your yarn, you have more latitude for pricing than you have with skeins of yarn. For one thing, yarn is not considered an *end product*. It may be handcrafted, but it is not clearly the final craft product, so its price is, like many other supplies, determined partly according to supply and demand. Besides that, yarn is priced partly in keeping with the "going price" of like commodities. Because it is an easily recognized and defined item, it is subject to competitive pricing.

Pricing Limitations

1. Part of your pricing should take into account what it would cost custom-

ers to be able to use your yarn. Be realistic about its value to them—for knitting or weaving things for themselves, or for using in items that they could then sell at a profit.

2. Price cannot be completely dependent on an hourly wage. When you are a beginner, you cannot expect to get paid more per pound of yarn just because it takes you longer to spin it than an experienced spinner would take. When you are faster, you then will be getting more per hour on the same yarn price per ounce or pound.

3. An hourly wage often must be a compromise between what you would *like* to make, what you *need* in order to get by, and what is *reasonable* considering the time and energy you devote to your work.

4. You may have to settle for what appears to be a fair price per ounce relative to what most other spinners charge. It could be considered overpriced by the customer if it is way out of line with the current price charged by others.

5. Your yarn or handspun article may not sell if it is overpriced in relation to its *sales appeal*. Most people do not buy handspun just because the spinner or the shop tells them it is handspun. They usually buy because it is attractive in terms of its high quality, color range, texture, or even its packaging or labeling, or some combination of these. The yarn that seems hardest to sell, in almost all areas of the country, is yarn that looks too much like machine-made yarn.

6. Remember that you still have to compete, at least on one level, with machine-made yarns or wovens of a similar nature. These yarns are usually labeled "homespun" even though they are factory made and would be much less misleading if called "homespun-type."

7. Even though you cannot charge "more than the market will bear," what the market will bear is different for different parts of the country. High density population is usually an indication of a high density of potential buyers. A shop that has a great number of customers, such as in an area with many tourists (or dense population), will have a lot of potential customers seeing your yarn, and can usually charge more per ounce knowing that a certain percentage of the customers will pay that price. The higher price you can get for your yarn in a densely populated area may be offset by a higher cost of living *if* you live in that area. If you live in the country, with a slightly lower cost of living, and sell your yarn through a shop in the city or by mail, then you may be able to turn the economics of these situations to your own advantage.

Pricing Considerations

Time

The time you spend includes buying, washing, sorting, and carding wool, as well as spinning and washing the spun yarn. It also includes time spent labeling and weighing yarn, corresponding with customers, keeping records (including balancing your checkbook), making business telephone calls, wrapping orders, and mailing and/or making deliveries to shops. Much of this time is nonproductive but a necessary part of business.

Materials

If the cost of materials is too high, the cost of making yarn increases, which cuts down on potential profit. Try to keep down the cost of materials by shopping wisely, buying in quantities, and using by-products (such as discarded wool for felting).

Overhead

The cost of maintaining the place where you work, which for most spinners is their home, is part of your overhead. A percentage of home costs can be deducted, according to strict rules, on your income tax. For the sake of simplicity in pricing, you can lump almost all business expenses other than the cost of fibers under the term of "overhead." This includes transportation, costs of making price lists, catalogs, and price tags, and so on.

On the plus side, take into consideration that you are able to work in your own home (even taking some of its expenses off

Samples of tags and skein bands.
Note that some skein bands have a
place for writing in the skein
weight and price. Hang tags,
without holes punched in them,
can serve as business cards.

your income tax), do not have to buy a special wardrobe to wear to a job, and do not have to hire a baby-sitter if you have small children. You are home when your children come home from school or when your spouse comes home from work or when a friend phones. Spinning, as a vocation, should put you where you *want* to be—home with your family or out in the country with your animals.

This does not mean you must work for nothing, but these are "fringe benefits" and to some people they are worth quite a bit. An "independent situation" carries more status these days than does a high paying job.

Income

Think "yearly income," not just hourly or weekly. One advantage of having to pay income tax is that it forces you to tally up all you took in and all your expenses for the year, and see how they add up.

Some yarn sizes or yarn items will be more profitable than others on an hourly-wage basis. Some things that take longer to make may have to be retailed for less than an article that takes less time, but this can average out to a fair wage when viewed as a total picture. Not putting all your eggs in one basket has an advantage. I am not advocating a jack-of-all-trades crafts approach, but a versatility *within* your spinning craft. In an emergency you can concentrate on the more profitable items you make or gradually work to eliminate the less profitable ones, unless you have some other reason for making them.

To make more profit you will need to work faster and/or more efficiently, or reduce your materials or overhead costs.

Underpricing

In fairness to yourself and to other working craftsmen, do not underprice. There is an old saying that if you lose five cents on every sale, you cannot make it up in volume.

Beginners may be tempted to underprice the going cost of handspun in order to get yarn orders more easily. In the beginning when they may have some other income and are just spinning to earn "extra" money, this works fine. But if sales are so good that they quit their regular job to spin full time, they can discover that they are not making a living

wage, even by working extra long hours.

Brucie Adams, an experienced spinner and shop owner, made a survey (published in *Interweave* magazine, winter 1978–1979) of thirty production spinners. It showed prices ranging from sixty cents an ounce to three dollars an ounce, but the area between one and two dollars accounted for almost all the prices. Only two people had prices much under one dollar, only one person had a price over two dollars. While this did not cover all the spinners in the country who sell yarn, it does give some indication that there is a general price range to be taken into account.

Price Options for Yarn

One way of getting more per ounce is to establish different prices for different types of your yarn. For example, some spinners charge different prices for yarns that require varying amounts of spinning time (such as one-ply, two-ply, novelty or fancy, vegetable dyed, and chemical dyed yarn) and yarns made from raw materials that vary in price (such as natural white yarn, natural medium shades, natural darker shades, and exotic fibers).

Price Options for Other Items

There is more flexibility in the pricing of finished items made from your handspun yarn, but it is not always easy to decide how far to carry the process. In some instances, there is a need not to sell too soon, if one more step will double your income from the same amount of raw material. While the actual cost of the material is important, the determining factors are the added time needed to produce the items and how readily they sell. In making any products from your yarn, you must watch out for diminishing returns. On some things you can still get more money by not carrying the process too far. For instance, because of the time element in the knitting of socks, especially in turning heels, it may be more profitable to sell a knitting pack of yarn and directions than to knit socks for sale—or to weave yardage but not tailor it, just sell the fabric; or to sell sweater yarn but not knit sweaters. Try to sell at the stage where you feel you are getting the most return for your effort.

Selling

Much of the appeal of handspinning as a livelihood is that it lends itself to a personal and independent way of living. But this presupposes a regular and consistent pattern of selling.

Although you may begin with an occasional sale, ultimately what you need is a way of methodically marketing your yarn, so you need to consider various ways of selling in light of your own specific situation. Look for the way that is most suitable for you considering such things as your family obligations and where you live. Mail order, for example, is always a convenient way of doing business, but it may be the only way if you live in a remote area. What could be a liability frequently becomes an asset when fully exploited. A long uninterrupted winter, for instance, could result in a tremendous amount of yarn and other items for spring and summer craft fairs.

Consignment

In consignment selling, you do not get paid until a shop sells your merchandise, so what are the advantages of consignment?

1. If you do not have ready cash sales for as much yarn as you can produce, it is better to have your yarn displayed in shops, with a chance to sell, than on the shelf at home.
2. When you *begin to sell* your yarn, consignment allows you to become known and established, because shops will take a chance on your yarn if they do not have to spend money in advance.
3. You get more cash in relation to the retail price—usually sixty to seventy percent of the price rather than the customary fifty percent for cash purchases. Sometimes a shop may be happy to pay cash, but sales are so brisk that it is to your advantage to keep selling on consignment.
4. It gives you a flexibility of inventory. You can take back items if you have an order from a gallery or a shop that pays cash for them.

For us, it worked out well to put yarn on consignment when we were first starting to sell, while also working toward a goal of eventually selling wholesale and retail for cash.

Limited Consignment

If you do not have adequate cash sales for your yarn and feel you should try consignment, consider a limited, time-trial arrangement with a shop or shops that seem genuinely interested in your yarn. Allow a shop to have an ample supply of your yarn on consignment with the understanding that it is for a three-month trial period, with payment at the end of each month for yarn sold in that month (the common method of payment). During that time, you should keep them well stocked, if the yarn is selling, so that their sales continue to be good. At the end of three months, if sales were brisk, you will have realized three sizable commission payments and the shop will be assured that their customers appreciate your yarn and will buy it at their price.

It should be understood in advance that at the end of the trial period all unsold yarn will be returned or purchased, and if they want to stock your yarn in the future, it will be purchased outright. If it has not sold well in that particular shop, they will not want to buy it, and you certainly will not want to continue leaving it there if it is not selling. You may have to try several shops before you find the best outlet for you.

Another way to try consignment would be for classes in weaving schools, colleges that have weaving classes, and weaving workshops. This can also be timed consignment if the classes are offered regularly throughout the year. Smaller skeins, such as one ounce, are most salable for classes because their projects are usually small.

Woven and Knitted Articles

Once the sales potential for your handspun yarn has been established, it can be assumed that subsequent orders will also be salable, so a shop may be willing to purchase outright. Items that are woven or knitted from handspun, however, are not in exactly the same category. With such merchandise, a shop still can be unsure that every item will be sold readily, and for that reason they often will be reluctant to tie up their money in them, favoring consignment. Selling yarn is like selling lumber; selling wovens or knits is like selling furniture. Yarn can be used in numerous ways, whereas wovens or knits can be used in relatively few ways.

Consignment Prices per Ounce

With any consignment of yarn, you may want to price it according to the scarcity of the color—a higher price per ounce on the more choice shades. Otherwise, customers can skim off the interesting shades and you will be left with the drab ones. When there is a price difference, I have noticed that customers take a better look at the lesser priced shades. They find ways to use them, yet still buy the nicer shades, too.

Consignment Contracts or Agreements

Whether doing limited or regular consignment, you should have a written contract or agreement. Many shops have a formal printed consignment memorandum that covers all types of craft merchandise, if they are doing primarily a consignment business.

A consignment contract or agreement should explain the shop's payment policy. Ordinarily, shops pay at the end of every month for all merchandise sold during that month. If you do not receive an expected payment at the proper time, check with the shop. If no merchandise has sold in a month, consider removing it in order to try it in other places.

The agreement should state the shop's degree of responsibility in case of loss from fire or theft. Some places are fully covered by insurance. Others are covered for fire but not theft, but are very careful with their merchandise and have a policy of reimbursing the craftsmen for a certain percentage of the value of the merchandise (usually fifty percent) in case of loss.

This excellent consignment agreement is a format suggested by Michael Scott, editor of The Crafts Report. *It is taken from* The Crafts Business Encyclopedia, *copyright © 1977 by Michael Scott. Reprinted by permission of Harcourt Brace Jovanovich, Inc.*

CONSIGNMENT MEMORANDUM

Date _____

1) Consignor: John Craftsperson
   _____ address

2) Consignee: Jane Merchant
   _____ address

3) Goods Consigned: The articles listed below and additional articles to be listed on consignor's invoices from time to time:

Quantity	Item	Retail Price on % to Consignee	(or)	Price to Consignee
_____	____	_____		_____

4) Accountings: Consignee will furnish a listing of items sold and price each month, together with a check for the purchase price. Consignor may check inventory at any time during normal business hours.

5) Risk of Loss: Goods lost, stolen or damaged will be treated as if sold.

6) Returns: Unsold goods in good condition may be returned at any time by consignee, and will be returned at consignor's request.

7) Other Provisions: (Insert provisions as to insurance, compliance with Uniform Commercial Code, or other special provisions which may be required).

8) Signatories:

_____
John Craftsperson

_____
Jane Merchant

The GOOD YEARS

GALLERIE and GARRET

OLD MILLTOWN

EDMONDS, WASHINGTON 98020

774-3050

CONSIGNMENT AGREEMENT

The undersigned artist consigns the following to THE GOOD YEARS GALLERIE, doing business in Edmonds, Washington, for sale at the retail price indicated (see attached artist receipt and inventory listing for items   #_____ to _____).

All items are to be delivered to THE GOOD YEARS at the artist's risk and expense. On or before the 10th day of the month following the month in which the item is sold, the artist shall receive _____ % of the retail price.

If any item is not sold within _____ days of receipt by THE GOOD YEARS, it shall be removed by or returned to the artist at the risk and expense of the artist unless a new consignment agreement is signed. Items shall be picked up on _____ , 197_____ . During an exhibition items may not be removed from the gallerie.

Items on consignment with THE GOOD YEARS shall be insured by the gallerie against vandalism, fire and extended coverage at the amount of the artist's commission. Items are/ are not covered by the artist's floating insurance policy. Items consigned to the gallerie are/ are not covered by copyright and/or patent laws.

Photographs or other reproductions of the artist's works may be made for purposes of newspaper advertising, catalog printing, handouts and other advertising.

The artist does/does not agree to further reproduction of works for sale in the form of post cards, calendars, graphics; providing that the artist shall receive 10% of the net profit of those sales at the end of the fiscal year of sales.

For exhibitions the artist agrees to pay for the items checked below:

_____ advertising $_____

_____ post cards $_____

_____ catalogs $_____

_____ Opening expenses in an amount not

   greater than _____ to include:

The title to the consigned items is considered to be held by the artist (or shipper) until sold.

The artist does/does not agree to sending of work consigned to THE GOOD YEARS to other galleries.

Accepted this _____ day of _____ , 197___ .

_____
Artist or authorized agent

_____
Gallerie Representative

Very detailed consignment contract. Note the mention of insurance and copyrights and/or patents.

If the shop is not in your area, the agreement also should specify who will pay the postage or freight on shipments to the shop and on return shipments of your merchandise if the shop decides to return it.

The pricing policy also should be spelled out. The usual practice is that the craftsman sets the retail price and the shop takes a fixed percentage of that price as a sales commission. This is the policy you can expect for skeins of yarn and with small items made from your yarn.

On a high-priced woven item, some galleries will have you set a minimum selling price. This allows them to price it at whatever amount above that price they think they can actually get from their customers as long as they pay you the agreed percentage on the actual selling price.

Consignment Record Keeping

Successful consignment selling requires a lot more bookkeeping than regular wholesaling does. You will need to keep a detailed record, for each shop, of all the merchandise you send, the date you send it, the date the shop receives it, the date you receive payment (remember to cross off the sold items), and the dates you receive any returned merchandise. When mailing consignment items, enclose a duplicate "packing slip/ receipt" and ask the shop to sign it and return it to you. If you have any reservations about mail being safely delivered to a shop, then insure the package you send and get a return receipt from the post office. For hand-delivered orders, make a list of the items or total weight of the yarn and ask the shop to sign it. Keep this, and the other receipts, on file.

Once or twice a year, reconcile your inventory with each shop that sells your merchandise. Send them a statement of what yarn or items you show as not being sold or returned. This can sometimes result in a payment for things sold but not yet reported, or items lost and covered by insurance. If you terminate a consignment arrangement with a shop, check your records against what they send back to you to be sure all unsold items are returned. Without efficient record keeping on your part, you might be unaware of lost or unpaid items.

Credit Checking

When a shop asks you to sell to them or put merchandise on consignment, it is not impolite to ask them for credit references and the names of several other craftsmen who do business with them. You can write to these people and ask how long they have done business with this shop and how prompt the shop is with payments.

Some craftsmen deal only with shops that have been established for at least two years, figuring that by then the shop is on a sound enough financial basis that they probably will not go out of business suddenly. If a shop does go broke, it frequently means that every bit of money they took in has been spent in the attempt to stay in business. It then may not be possible for a craftsman to get payment for sold merchandise, and even unsold merchandise may not be retrievable. This is one reason you should be sure you get each monthly check on time and investigate if you think your merchandise has been sold and you have not received a payment. Several states have consignment legislation pending that would give specific protection to artists and craftsmen.

Exclusives

Some places ask for an exclusive in their area, which often can be of advantage to you, also. It is better to have a good inventory in one shop than to scatter your products around in too many shops. It is also better to have yarn in several shops in different areas than in several in one town. (Refer to the treatment of exclusives in the "Wholesale" section.)

Merchandise Rotation

Rotate woven or knitted things that do not sell in a reasonable length of time. They may sell quite well when displayed and lighted differently or in another shop that has different customers. When you find the shop that does best with each particular item, keep them well supplied.

Import Problems

I used to feel quite strongly that a spinner should not do a consignment business with any shop that paid cash for the imported handspun yarn they stocked. I had several reasons for feeling that way:

1. They always have more incentive to encourage sales of the yarn in which their money is already invested.
2. They usually sell the imports for less because of the standard of living in the country of origin. A shop could use the higher price of domestic yarn to help sell the imported yarn by showing the customer it is a "bargain."
3. If a shop can expect sales of handspun yarn, it is unfair that they pay cash for imported yarn and take advantage of a local spinner's willingness to deal on consignment.

While I still think it is unfair to you if they pay cash for imported handspun and want yours on consignment, it may sometimes be necessary to make a consignment arrangement *for a trial period of time* in order to demonstrate that your yarn is salable on a competitive basis with the imports.

Most spinning-weaving shops now sell both imported and domestic handspun, and are having good sales in both. In most instances, their domestic handspun is obviously of higher quality and well worth the difference in price.

Wholesale

Since it means accepting a lower price per pound than retail, why should spinners want to sell their yarn wholesale? Since I am one who prefers wholesaling, it is not hard to give the reasons.

For one thing, you do not have to spend as much time in correspondence (nonproductive time) or in estimating your customer's needs for a specific knitting or weaving project, or spend time in person with customers in your shop, when you need the spinning time to fill orders.

Shop orders are easier to fill than retail orders, as shops usually order by pounds rather than a few ounces of one color and a few ounces of another color. Yarn size is not so crucial, and colors are usually specified only approximately, if at all. You also do not have to spend more time traveling to craft fairs and trying to sell to customers than you spend spinning.

What do retailers do that they should make as much per ounce as you do? They pay you in advance, taking the risk that the yarn will sell and that the customer's check will clear the bank. They take the loss in case of shoplifting or damage to the merchandise. They carry expensive insurance to protect against the customer who might be injured on the premises. They spend the time with prospective customers, time that does not always result in a sale. They keep regular shop hours, which would be very confining for you to do in your own studio. They pay the rent, utility bills, and clerks' salaries, as well as the costs of business licenses, advertising, display cases, telephone business listings, and so on.

Where

The attitude of the people who own or run a shop is one indication of that store's potential for selling your yarn. If they are pleased with it, they will not only give it choice display space, but also will bring it to the customer's attention, telling about the spinner, about the uniqueness of this particular yarn, and about how fortunate they are to have it in their shop. The customer responds to this enthusiasm by purchasing the yarn.

When you offer your yarn to various shops and one seems reluctant, telling you they doubt that their customers would be interested, do not coax them or suggest they try it on consignment. Look for the shop or shops that will be delighted with it.

A yarn or spinning-weaving shop is usually a better outlet for handspun yarn than a general gift shop or a shop that carries a great variety of handcrafts. There are exceptions to this, such as in a tourist area, but on the whole, a higher percentage of yarn shop customers can be expected to be interested in handspun since they are specifically interested in yarn.

Another exception are places where your yarn or woven item is among "good company." The customers at a prestigious gallery or craft shop are usually different from those at a craft fair, your studio-shop, or a small yarn or weaving shop. Even if a big volume of your work does not sell at a gallery or special shop, you may be able to make contacts that will result in commissions for larger and more expensive articles.

How

Be sure to quote the same wholesale price to all shops. If you give an extra discount for larger quantities, offer it to all out-

Fleeces and spinning wheels in a gallery's "Loom Room," a separate building housing spinning and weaving equipment. (Bonneville Gallery in Gig Harbor, Washington)

lets. Requiring a minimum initial order will tend to restrict sales to those shops that have the most sincere interest in selling your yarn. No minimum is usually stipulated on reorders, but it is on the reorders that you may want to give extra discounts on orders for larger quantities. You could ask for advance notice on orders, such as two weeks before expected delivery. If you are unable to supply the yarn at once, then acknowledge the order with a delivery date. Also encourage the shop to reorder before their stock is depleted. A scant display of yarn does not sell as well as a profusion of yarn.

Have clear business terms, such as who pays the freight or postage. If your situation makes it important for you to be paid promptly, you could encourage this by prepaying the postage on paid-in-advance orders, and billing the customer for postage on all orders that require invoices.

The fewer conditions, such as color choices and skein size, that a shop requests in their orders, the easier it is to fill their orders and thus the more profitable it is. If you are spinning natural sheep shades or vegetable dyed colors, you may want to offer only "assorted" colors, with no color choice. You also may want to tell the shop that you cannot match any of these colors. The shop must tell their customers that these are all one-of-a-kind shades and cannot be matched.

Once a shop has your yarn, help them sell it. Be sure they know all about it—for example, whether or not it is preshrunk and washable; whether the colors are natural sheep shades, natural dyed shades, or chemical dyed shades; and what size knitting needles should be used. This information also could be on the yarn label. You can help the shop with display tips, such as mentioning that handwoven items used as a backdrop for pottery do not sell well. At the same time, the shop may advise you about how to enhance the appeal of your yarn or other products.

Suggested Retail Price

Your retail price direct to customers ideally should be the same price as that of stores who are retailing your yarn. But, in selling outright to stores you can specify only a "suggested retail." If they think they can charge more and get it, and are not too close to where you are selling from your studio,

then that is for them to determine. You can sell for your "suggested retail" price even though they choose to price it higher.

I find that customers will pay more for my yarn in a shop than they would pay if they ordered directly from me, and some of them *know* they are paying more. But in the shop they can pay the price and get instant delivery, while they might have to wait four to six weeks if they ordered from me by mail.

Credit Terms

On the initial order from a new account, some craftsmen request payment in advance, particularly if they are not acquainted with the shop owner or do not know other craftsmen who sell to that shop. It also is not out of line to ask for credit references—the names of several other craftsmen from whom the shop purchases yarn or other items.

On reorders from an established account, an invoice is sent at the time of the shipment of their order, and payment is expected within thirty days. We have found that a majority of our customers pay in less than thirty days.

Exclusives

Should you give an exclusive sales agreement to a shop, letting them be the only shop in the area to carry your yarn? While this is advantageous, it is not safe to get talked into an exclusive agreement with a shop until you are certain they can do a good job of selling your yarn. Even then, it should be with the understanding that it is based on good sales and repeat orders.

Having an exclusive can give a shop an extra inducement to promote your yarn, knowing that in doing so they are increasing their own sales and not helping a competitor who also sells your yarn. For the spinner, it is advantageous to sell to only one shop in a certain area, giving them good delivery and working to help them achieve a high volume of sales.

Getting a request for an exclusive arrangement can give you the opportunity to bargain, such as suggesting a monthly or bimonthly shipment. Some of the shops that carry our yarn have a standing order to be sent on a regular basis. This keeps them reliably supplied without delays, and enables us to routinely work their orders into our schedule.

Studio-Shop

The midway position between selling to retail shops and opening a retail shop of your own is having a shop in your home. Selling from your "studio" lets you work at spinning and your other work when there are no customers, saves commuting time to a separate shop, and still gives you complete control over the display and pricing of your merchandise. It avoids the payment of commissions for consignment selling and the discount given to wholesale buyers. Part of your everyday home expenses will be tax deductible as business expenses—lights, water, phone, heat, and so on. Be sure to keep accurate records on the total amounts of these in order to take the allowable percentage of deduction.

For either a home shop or one that is separate, you must set some business hours and then follow them in order to keep your customers. This is more confining than mail order, but if you do not keep regular hours, customers may not return after finding you closed when you were supposed to be open.

You will have many interruptions from the telephone and from customers, and some lookers without any intention of buying, so you may have to put in some long hours, spinning your yarn when your shop is closed. An "open by appointment" policy can reduce the number of casual shoppers and give more freedom in planning your

An inexpensive arrangement for displaying fleeces for sale in a small shop. (The Shearing Shed, Sisters, Oregon)

activities. It is a good way to start, even if you eventually plan on keeping regular business hours.

Your Own Shop

For a successful retail shop, location is important. But whether you select an idyllic setting that will lure tourists, a busy street that has many shoppers, or an artist-colony area where people look for crafts, try to open in a place that will be permanent. It is bad for business, and sometimes damaging to your craftsman image, to change from place to place. Customers may think that you are unreliable or that your business has failed if they find your shop has moved.

It is hard to start any shop without an initial capital investment. For one thing, you can count on a lot of additional monthly expenses, such as display lighting (some must be left on at night), rent, phone, heat, fire insurance, personal liability insurance, advertising, sales check forms, tape, tissue, and other small necessities, in addition to the initial purchase of fixtures and signs. In order to keep a good credit rating, you must pay these and all other shop bills promptly.

Check all your advertising, especially "Yellow Pages" listings, to ensure that your correct address and phone number are listed under the proper heading. The first year The Shearing Shed in Sisters, Oregon, was in business, the telephone company listed it under "Barber Shops" in the "Yellow Pages." Later it was moved to "Beauty Parlors," which was not much better. As this is the only spinning-weaving shop within a large area, the error was understandable, but resulted in a loss of valuable advertising.

Adequate production may be another problem. It takes a great bulk of yarn and other items to stock even a small shop, and if you plan to manufacture all your own merchandise, you will find it difficult to keep up if sales are good. If sales are not good, you will just have a hard time staying in business. To get an idea of the requirements, figure out how much yarn you would have to sell each day in order that the amount of *profit* on that quantity would more than cover the rent and all the additional expenses. Can you actually produce that much and still operate a shop? Remember, it would have to be way beyond that in order to make a living or even do much more than break even.

One option is to sell other people's crafts as well and either specialize in selling handspun or branch out into crafts in general. This requires knowledge and good judgment in order to select salable items and turn away tactfully what you believe will not sell. You cannot afford to give shop space, even on a consignment basis, to items that have too slow a turnover.

If you open a retail shop, there is a good chance that you will end up being a shopkeeper, an accountant, and a salesclerk, and will no longer have any time at all for spinning. Even if the shop prospers, you could still have failed in the original goal of having a store to sell your own yarn.

Most shops that have opened with the primary intent of selling the owner's yarn have branched next into selling spinning supplies, then to including weaving supplies, then to having equipment and classes. Linda Woods of the Country Weaver in Puyallup, Washington, was teaching spinning before opening her shop, and found that the classes not only provide income in the shop, but also generate business in equipment and supplies. She started with only $2,000 and for the first two years reinvested all of the profits back into shop inventory. The smaller the initial investment, the longer a shop can anticipate having to put all income back into it.

A new shop has to face competition from similar shops within driving distance; from mail-order shops that do a volume business by catalog and can usually undersell small shops; and from cheap imports, primitive handspun, and imitation handspun (called "homespun") sold through shops all over the country. Even with sufficient capital to finance the first year or two, it still will take a combination of excellent craftsmanship, efficient business management, and specialized customer relations for a shop to survive.

Shop Partnership

One way to minimize the investment and the amount of time spent in a shop is to have a partner. This arrangement may sound ideal at first, but it does have many potential problems.

A legal partnership entails legal obligations, such as assuming individual responsibility for the total debts should your partner die or leave suddenly. In most states, you can consider establishing a "limited partnership," which prevents personal property from being seized in order to satisfy the debts of a partnership. The death of either partner also can create a financial snarl, but the money needed to unravel it can be anticipated by each partner having life insurance made out to the other partner.

Partnerships, whether legally established or informally shared by friends, should have a written agreement that spells out how the partnership will function. For example, the agreement should state not only the number of hours each partner will work, but also who will open and who will close the store, and how vacations are to be handled. It should explain what will be done if one of the partners should want to leave—will that partner's half revert to the other without payment or upon repayment of the initial investment, or can the shop be sold to someone else? And if it is sold, who gets to choose the person who buys it? The remaining partner may not enjoy suddenly having a total stranger for a new "partner." (This has been known to happen.)

Mail Order

Handspun yarn is a convenient item to sell by mail. Yarn sample cards can be sent through the mail without any problem of weight, bulkiness, or fragility. Although merchandising woven items is a bit more difficult, clear photos or stylish drawings, along with samples of the yarn used to make them, can produce good results.

Selling by mail has all the tax advantages of a shop in your home, without the extra expenses of display cases and other shop niceties. Because customers will not be coming to your door, you can work and live where you wish, even in a remote area. You can maintain the privacy of your family life and have time to fill your yarn orders, working during hours that are convenient for you.

On the other hand, quite a bit of time is involved in mailing out orders, but this can be consolidated into a certain part of the day (or every other day) to be more efficient. Mailing chores are simplified if all your boxes, tissue, string, and marking pens are in a "shipping area." Keep plenty of white tissue on hand, for use in packing the yarn.

This makes the shipment more attractive and protects the yarn from the box. It also conveys the impression that you care and that the contents are valuable.

Keep a collection of corrugated boxes so that you can easily find the right size box for each order. Check often with local merchants for boxes, and especially look for boxes without much printing on them. With yarn, pack the contents so that the box is reasonably full, to prevent it from being crushed. Textiles can be rolled on cardboard rollers (discards from fabric stores), wrapped with tissue and then with heavy brown paper, and then taped closed.

Try to do a neat job of taping and tying boxes, as the professional appearance of the package is an important part of your image. Use strong tape on the box, so that it can withstand rough handling en route.

Use a waterproof marking pen to address the parcel; a damp address can smear and become illegible. Insure valuable packages and shipments that you are sending to possibly unsafe delivery locations, such as apartment houses. Country addresses with route numbers and box numbers are less risky, and addresses with post office box numbers are even safer because the packages will be staying in a safe place until the customers pick them up.

For tax purposes, have the post office give you a receipt, stamped with the date, for stamps and postage. Postage is a large expense in a mail-order business, and you may need to substantiate the amount claimed on your income tax return.

The words "mail order" may bring visions of mailing thousands of catalogs to names on a purchased mailing list. That approach is valid for a merchant who is purchasing products and reselling them, but not for a spinner. Because of the relatively limited quantity of yarn one person can turn out, expensive ads or large bulk mailings are not only unnecessary, but also could lead to a deluge of orders that could not be filled.

You can let business grow gradually by depending on word-of-mouth recommendations from satisfied customers. Or you can take out an inexpensive classified ad, offering your sample card, in one of the spinning-weaving publications (see "Sources" chapter). Have a few dozen cards made up in advance, so you will be prepared in case you get an avalanche of requests, and be sure to charge a fee that will at least compensate you for time, yarn, and postage.

Business done by mail can be retail or wholesale or both. Wholesale outlets could be located by sending yarn samples and prices to the spinning-weaving shops that advertise in weaving publications. Give full details in your first contact so that a shop could place an order based on the information you sent them. You should state who will pay postage and insurance, how skeins are labeled, minimum initial order that will be accepted, and payment terms. Give an estimated delivery time, and when you get a shop order, acknowledge it and give an amended delivery date, if necessary. One buyer of fiber crafts, Pat Foley of Contemporary Fibre Design (Portland, Maine), has said, "We need a more professional attitude among handspinners offering their yarns for sale. It is hard to get orders filled at all, let alone on time."

Selling by mail means a lot of corresponding with customers, so decide if you are good at answering letters. If not, maybe someone in your family might enjoy it. If you are a procrastinator about writing and prefer dealing directly with customers, then your own studio-shop or retail shop may be the way to go.

Price List

Your price list represents you and your work, especially to people whose only contact with you is through your price list. It should be attractive and distinctively yours, and it should include the following information:

1. Your name and address, including the zip code
2. Your design logo, if you have one
3. The price of your sample card
4. Yarn prices per ounce and/or per pound for different sizes or types of yarn
5. Quantity discount price, if you have one
6. Statement of postage charges
7. Prices of items made from your yarn, if you make any
8. Prices for books or supplies, if you sell them
9. Cost of lessons or classes, if you teach
10. Notation of sales tax to be added by state residents, if this applies

If you anticipate or are seeking wholesale inquiries, then consider the possibility of showing wholesale prices down the left edge of the page, corresponding to the line of retail prices on the opposite side. This saves the cost of printing two separate price lists, as you can just trim off the wholesale prices when you send the list to retail customers.

Sample Card

Your sample card should provide the following information so that a customer without a price list can still place an order:

1. Your name and address, including the zip code

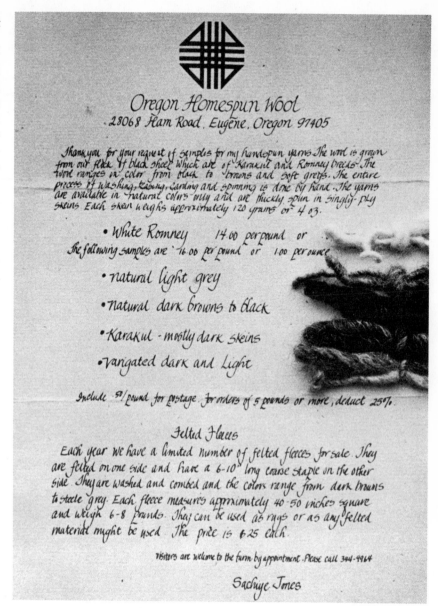

Sample card, including information about felted fleeces from Karakul-Romney sheep. (Sachiye Jones, Eugene, Oregon)

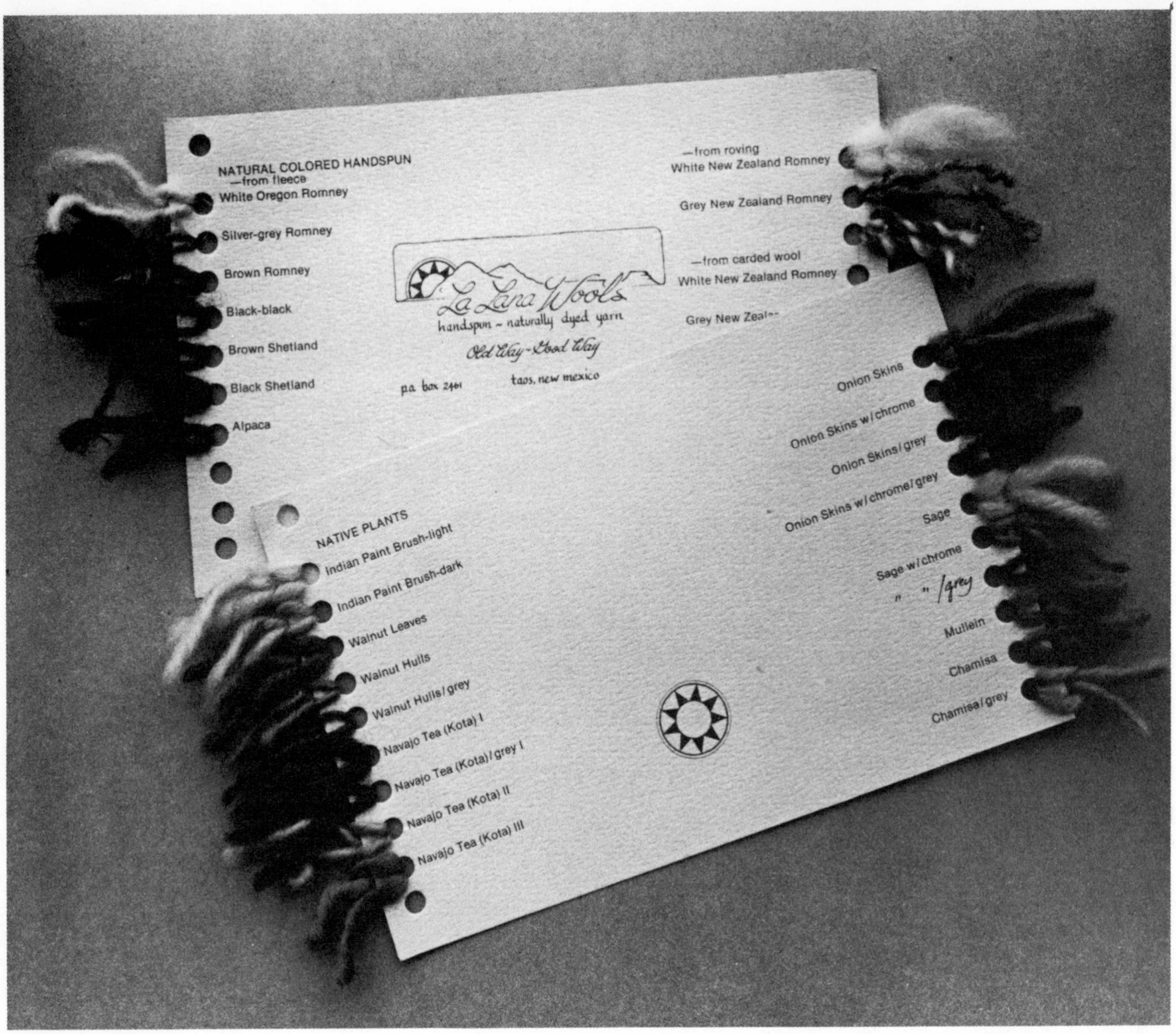
NATURAL COLORED HANDSPUN
—from fleece
White Oregon Romney
Silver-grey Romney
Brown Romney
Black-black
Brown Shetland
Black Shetland
Alpaca
La Lana Wools
handspun ~ naturally dyed yarn
Old Way - Good Way
p.o. box 2461
taos, new mexico
—from roving
White New Zealand Romney
Grey New Zealand Romney
—from carded wool
White New Zealand Romney
NATIVE PLANTS
Indian Paint Brush-light
Indian Paint Brush-dark
Walnut Leaves
Walnut Hulls
Walnut Hulls/grey
Navajo Tea (Kota) I
Navajo Tea (Kota)/grey I
Navajo Tea (Kota) II
Navajo Tea (Kota) III
Onion Skins
Onion Skins w/chrome
Onion Skins/grey
Onion Skins w/chrome/grey
Sage
Sage w/chrome
" " /grey
Mullein
Chamisa
Chamisa/grey

Two of four yarn sample cards sent out by two spinners who do all their business by mail. (La Lana Wools, Taos, New Mexico)

2. Your design logo
3. Yarn snips
4. Yarn prices. (If you have various prices for different yarn sizes or types, then list the price next to the corresponding sample.)
5. Approximate delivery time
6. Ordering instructions, such as "Give first and second color choice" or "Return entire yarn snip of color ordered"
7. Notation as to quantities available, if they are limited
8. Warning, if necessary, that colors are one of a kind and that the customer must order enough at one time to complete a project

Writing of the above information on each sample card does not look as professional as when you have it printed. The cheapest way is to type out the information quite a few times on eight and one-half by eleven-inch white paper, then have this printed, slightly reduced in size, by offset. You then can cut the information slips apart and tape one to each sample card. By doing this, you have a legible and informative label for each card, and can use any available type of inexpensive cardboard, punched with a hand punch, for sample cards. You may eventually want to invest in a more impressive card, after experimenting long enough to decide the exact wording you want to use on it and how many yarn samples you want to put on each card.

Most spinners charge one or two dollars

for their sample card, some allowing this as a credit against the first yarn order in excess of ten dollars. Without a substantial charge for your yarn samples, you will find yourself spending a lot of unprofitable time in assembling them, for many requests for sample cards are from people who are just curious and not interested in actually buying.

TWEEDS: Preshrunk, natural color, handspun to order in random variegated shades. These are one-of-a-kind colors, cannot be matched, only approximated. Order sufficient at one time to complete project. To order, return entire yarn sample. Please indicate 1st and 2nd choice. Delivery 8-10 weeks, depending on orders ahead. Light and medium shades $1.35 per ounce plus postage; darker shades, due to limited supply, $1.70 per ounce plus postage.
PAULA SIMMONS, Box 12, SUQUAMISH, WASH. 98392

Catalog

If you have sufficient orders flowing in to keep you busy, a simple price list and sample card may be all you need to sustain your business. A catalog is justified only if your production capacity warrants the expense and/or you make a variety of woven, knitted, or crocheted articles from your yarn that can be marketed by mail only with a catalog.

Catalog Illustrations or Photos

A catalog stimulates sales only if items are portrayed attractively, so the illustrations or photos should be of professional quality, but this does not mean "slick." If you use drawings, they should all be done by the same person, in the same style, to give a coordinated look to the catalog. Line drawings reproduce well, but must be done in black ink. (Blue does not reproduce well.)

In an inexpensive printing job, photographs will not come out quite as clear as they were in the original, but if they are good closeup photos and large enough, they usually will be satisfactory. If all your photos have a white background, you could ask the printer to bleed out the edges; in other words, have the white of the background blend into the white of the page, so that the page does not appear to have a square photo inset in it. When a photo does not have a white background, there is a simple solution: carefully cut out the image of the merchandise from the photo, then darken the cut edge with a felt-tip pen (black or dark gray) so the photo does not look like it was cut out. You then can paste this trimmed photograph onto the typed or typeset page, and it is ready for printing.

Some printers, for an extra charge, will "screen" photos. This reduces the photo image to a pattern of tiny dots, which allows better reproduction.

Catalog Pages

Having a loose-leaf catalog that is stapled together allows you to add or delete pages, change your price list, and enter seasonal promotions. You can print catalog pages on standard twenty-pound, white bond paper, if you are printing on one side only; use a little heavier paper if it will be

Slips that are taped to yarn sample cards to provide ordering information.

Loose-leaf catalog page, with hand lettering and pen-and-ink drawings. (Sachiye Jones, Eugene, Oregon)

The Long Tunic

Very warm overgarment made of natural dark handspun & two-ply Canadian wool warp. The sleeves are trimmed in bright natural dyed handspun. Size is 60 inches from sleeve to sleeve & body is 50 inches around & 38 to 40 inches long. Fringe is braided or twined.

printed on both sides. The cover folder will need sturdier paper, and should include your logo, name, and address.

Merchandise presentation is most effective when you have a separate page for each item produced. Do not allow a page to get crowded or cluttered; work for a simple and stylized look. Each page should have an illustration or photo; the name of the item; the type of materials used, such as handspun wool warp and weft, natural color or vegetable dyed handspun; the sizes available, if the item comes in more than one size; the dimensions for such items as a couch throw, baby blanket, or poncho; the choice of colors; and the delivery time. For a successful standard item, print large quantities of the page (without a price on it) so the supply will last for several years. (Quantity printing costs less per sheet.) If the item is still experimental, print a more limited number.

With the price list on a separate page, you can change prices and postage charges as needed. The same catalog can also be used for either retail or wholesale.

Catalog Size

Since this catalog will be going through the mail, you need to size it conveniently, either to fit into a standard long envelope when folded, or to go through the mail without an envelope, or to fit into an inexpensive, lightweight, standard-sized mailer.

Offset printing is your best value for catalog reproduction, and standard eight and one-half by eleven-inch letterhead is the least expensive offset page size. It is a little large for a catalog that uses a separate page for each item, since you will be paying by the ounce to mail it, but that standard size can make up as a double page folded in the center, which results in two individual pages of five and one-half by eight and one-half inches each. For completely separate pages, just cut them in the center instead of folding them. The next most convenient size for printing is "legal" size or eight and one-half by fourteen inches, which when folded or cut in half makes two pages, each seven by eight and one-half inches. (This is the size I used for my *Patterns for Handspun* booklet, having the pages cut rather than folded.)

Catalog Printing

For the best printing price, pages should be "camera ready." This means that the offset printer does not have to do anything except photograph them, print them, and cut the pages in half, if that is your plan. You must have the illustrations or photos properly placed where you want them and your lettering completed.

Most offset printers will reduce the size of your whole layout if you request it, and print it reduced, at no extra charge. Reducing will make a typed page look more like it was typeset, which means you can actually type out the text of your catalog rather than pay for typesetting. Use a new black typewriter ribbon (carbon ribbon reproduces better than fabric ribbon) and check carefully for mistakes. Some typewriters produce a more professional look than others, and some even have a type style that does not need reduction.

Paste-on lettering, which is fairly easy to use and available in a wide variety of styles, is especially effective for the cover lettering, title page, and page headings. Referred to as "art type," it is sold in most art-supply stores. The other alternative is to letter the copy by hand. If you are good at calligraphy, then this could solve the lettering problem and would be very appropriate for presenting handspun.

Hand silk-screened brochure given out at craft fairs. These result in inquiries long after fairs are over—sometimes even years later.

Craft Fairs

While it is nice to work for yourself and not have to account for your time to someone else, it does present problems, for without deadlines and other commitments it sometimes is hard to be really productive. If you plan to attend craft fairs, then you will have some firm deadlines to meet.

Attending craft fairs is important for other reasons, too, especially if you are just starting to sell your yarn or other items. A fair exposes you to the public and provides an opportunity to hand out price lists, business cards, or brochures of some kind. By meeting your potential customers, you can gauge their reaction to your products, notice what they find attractive, see how garments fit them, and hear what they have to say about your prices. You also can explain your work to them, making them more informed and more appreciative of its quality. Some may not buy anything, but frequently they will call it to the attention of someone who will.

Fairs also give you a chance to meet other craftsmen and observe how they handle the public and how they solve such standard problems as how to display their wares and set up their booths. You also can pick up information about profitable fairs from craftsmen who have had personal experience with them, and discuss the reliability of potential retail outlets.

Fairs can fit into the plans of spinners who find it more convenient, because of climate, employment, or family circumstances, to spin only seasonally and then do all their selling at one time.

What to Look For

1. Established craft fairs. These have a good following and are usually more profitable for the craftsmen than newer fairs. The first year or two of any fair is when the organizers need to experiment to find more professional and effective ways of staging it.
2. Fairs that advertise. To attract customers, a good deal of advertising must be done, and in more than one media. The biggest fairs actually hire

Arrangement of folding screens used to display handspun yarn and inkle woven merchandise. The various fixtures that fit into pegboard are ideal for hanging skeins of yarn. (Arlene Graham, Bellevue, Nebraska)

Folding sections made from low-grade pine, weathered by being left outdoors for a winter. Several of these sections can be arranged to fit into any size fair booth and are used in a studio-shop the rest of the year. (Pat Foley, Portland, Maine)

public relations firms to coordinate their publicity and make sure the public knows the date and place, and hears plenty of interesting things about the fair.

3. Good attendance. For substantial sales you will want a fair that can show evidence, or has the reputation, of having high attendance and sales.

4. A juried fair. Once a fair has attracted enough craftsmen, a firm policy of screening all entries can be developed. When a fair has a reputation of having only high quality items, customers will be confident about spending money there. With items under five dollars, this may not make too much difference, but for larger sales it does.

5. A concern for craftsmen. This is evidenced by the fair's personnel being helpful, giving advance advice about the weather, specific display problems, banking facilities, security provisions, lodging, and so on.

6. Suitable size. Smaller fairs and those with a shorter history of operation usually will have the best sales on smaller items. Smaller skeins of yarn (thus costing less per skein) and smaller woven items (such as miniature tote bags instead of large couch throws) sell better at smaller fairs.

7. Appropriate season. A fair held during the fall, in theory, should allow better sales on woolens than a fair in mid-summer. Many interested potential buyers will not try on a wool garment in the heat of a July

fair. This does not mean that wool will not sell in the summer, but you can anticipate better sales in cooler weather.

What to Avoid

1. Fairs that charge admission. This may cut down on potential crowds. Some good fairs do charge, but be sure it is a fair that can still assure you of having a large attendance.

2. Shopping mall fairs. These fairs are supported by the mall merchants as a means of drawing the public to the area to spend money in the shops. The customary shoppers there are curious about but not particularly interested in crafts, so you will have a high percentage of people around who will not be actual customers. In addition, space is often more limited than at outdoor fairs, so setting up can be complicated both by lack of space and by mall regulations.

3. Fairs with high booth rentals. If the booth rental is high in relation to the quantity of merchandise you expect to have ready to sell, a fair will not be profitable for you. There are fairs that take only a commission based on sales. Then if you sell very little, the money you pay to the fair will also be small.

4. Fairs that are too far away. A fair too far from your home may prove unprofitable because of traveling time, which is also time lost from production, and the costs of lodging and meals. However, if you can call on shops along the way or have some other reason for making the trip, such a fair may be worth attending.

Craft booth module, consisting of folding screens with a shelf at counter height. The yarn racks at each end are designed to protect the skeins from shoplifting. (Linda Berry Walker, Kingston, New Jersey)

Booth Planning

Devise a simple background that can function also as an enclosure. Sets of folding panels could be bolted or hinged together for rigidity, and are versatile enough for use in different sized spaces. Some of your yarns or wovens could be hung or otherwise fastened to this background, as well as displayed on tables or shelves. Tables can be covered with burlap or other plain material, having enough overhang to allow concealed storage space beneath the tables. This gives you places for extra merchandise and for empty packing boxes.

Booth modules should be lightweight for packing, and easily assembled and taken down. That will make the transporting, setting up, and dismantling of your booth less hectic. The more efficiently you handle each part of the operation, the more successful the total effect will be.

Demonstrating

It has been our experience, and other spinners have noted the same thing, that you sell less when demonstrating. Even if you have someone to write up sales while you are spinning, you attract more lookers than buyers, and when you quit spinning, your audience just moves on. The larger sales are usually made when the crowd is thin and buyers can get your personal attention.

One fair we know takes this into account and allows demonstrators five dollars an hour credit against the commission to be collected on their sales. In effect, the spinner is paid five dollars for each hour spent demonstrating. While this does not necessarily make up for sales lost during that time, at least it shows that the management appreciates the people who do the entertaining that makes the whole fair more interesting.

Craft fair booth designed for selling looms as well as pillows and other articles woven of handspun. (Peter and Helga Reimers, Hinesburg, Vermont)

Some Other Tips

1. Have prices on the tags and attach them to the items you will be selling ahead of time. Attaching tags when the public is already crowding into your booth is almost impossible.

2. Have lots of merchandise. With plenty to choose from, customers can easily find something that suits them. Even with enough merchandise, when you get down to one or two of any particular item, it is unlikely to sell.

3. Try for at least one new type of item each year, if you make knitted or woven items from your yarn, so that customers from former years will notice the new pieces and not assume they have seen everything you make.

4. Display your items attractively and in a way that shows they are for sale. Merchandise that is arranged like an educational exhibit, showing various stages of processing, or like a collection of museum artifacts does not stimulate the viewer to spend money.

5. Avoid confusion in your display, for if it tires the potential customers to look at it, they will walk away.

6. Too elaborate a display appeals to the aesthetic nature rather than to acquisitiveness, and will draw more compliments than sales.

7. Develop a selling attitude for fairs, being friendly to the customers and anticipating the questions they invariably want to ask. The more they know about what you are doing, the better they can relate to your wares and the more inclined they are to buy.

8. Even if it is not a wholesaling type of fair, be prepared to talk with shop buyers, who normally frequent craft fairs to search for merchandise. Some are looking especially for crafts they can obtain on consignment, so decide what kind of consignment terms would interest you. Never promise more volume than you are sure you can produce.

9. Keep your cash box in a safe place, such as in a drawer. Put all large bills under the coin tray, and periodically transfer them to some place that is less accessible. If you have a bank stamp, put it on each check as you receive it. We send the stamped checks to the bank each day, then pay the fair's commission with cash, which cuts down on the amount of currency on hand.

10. Decide ahead of time whether you will sell large items on an installment plan, and whether you will add shipping charges to the price of orders you take for future delivery. Be prepared to quote your terms in a professional manner.

11. Give an estimated delivery time for orders, keeping track of the amount of orders taken, so that you can consider how many orders you have already when you give an approximate delivery date.

12. Put a price list and/or business card in the bag with each sale you make. Each customer is a potential future customer, and repeat orders are a good indication of satisfaction.

13. Keep a mailing list of craft fair customers. This is easily done for those who pay by check, and you can just ask buyers who pay cash to give you their names and addresses. This is doubly important if they are purchasing a high priced item. Later in the year or around Christmas shopping time, you can send a price list to everyone on your mailing list.

14. Publicize your spinning classes, if you teach, and sign up students during the fair.

15. Do not mark down merchandise prices in the last few hours of the fair. In many fairs this is against the rules, but even when it is permitted, the practice is most unbusinesslike and may result in buyers passing up your wares at the regular price and waiting for you to discount them at the close of a fair.

16. If you travel to quite a few fairs, compare the relative expenses and sales, and eliminate the less profitable ones. This will give you more working time to turn out merchandise for the others.

Customer Relations

In selling yarn, you are not selling something someone else made—you are selling something you made, so it lends itself to a personal involvement that is not found in purely commercial transactions. Even though it is a buyer-seller relationship, it goes far beyond that in terms of personal interest.

As a self-employed craftsman, your private life and your professional life are difficult to view separately. In both correspondence and in meeting the public, you have to keep in mind the customers' legitimate interest in the craftsman as a person. They are not buying a mass-produced item, but a particular piece of work done by a particular person. The money pays your bills, but the appreciation implicit in their willingness to buy is what really keeps you in business.

Special Help

If you know how to knit, weave, and crochet, you will be able to advise your customers regarding the use of your yarn for these purposes. If you do not, it could be well worth your while to learn, not just for the sake of your customers, but also to give yourself more alternatives for generating income.

If you sell yarn to weavers, it is important to have a working knowledge of weaving. Questions about how many threads to set per inch in their warp can be answered confidently only if you have woven with your yarn. You should also be able to give advice about sizing the warp yarn, about how much take-up to expect after weaving, and about washing the finished article.

Even more help may be needed by customers buying knitting or crocheting yarn. They are going to ask you to estimate the amount of yarn they will need for a garment of a certain size, and to suggest knitting needle and crochet hook sizes.

Knitting yarn customers often send the pattern they plan to use, asking you to spin up the size yarn needed for it and the quantity they should have. While commercial patterns give the amount of yarn needed in ounces or skeins, this weight holds true only for the brand and type of yarn mentioned in the pattern. (A pattern will usually require more ounces of handspun.) When a specific brand of yarn is mentioned, and you can find out the number of yards per skein or per ounce of that brand and type, then this could be translated into an equal number of yards of handspun. While the weight required may be different, the number of yards will be approximately the same.

Even if customers think they know how much they want, it pays to lay aside a few skeins, letting them know you will hold the matching yarn for a certain length of time, in case they need it. Give a specific cutoff date, and be sure they understand that they must let you know by that date if they need more yarn. Even after the cutoff date, I sometimes drop a card, reminding them to let me know if it appears they still might need the yarn. This is easier than having to try to match the color and yarn size at a later date, when they find they need another skein.

By knowing what a customer plans to do with the yarn they are ordering from you, it is possible to provide an added convenience—shipping the yarn in skeins to weavers and in center-pull balls to knitters.

For knitting and crocheting, yarn that has been washed in hot water and blocked to dry can be considered preshrunk. Including a printed slip of washing instructions with the order is useful and thoughtful. These instructions can point out that garments knitted from your yarn are hand washable, but should not be agitated in a washing machine or dried in a dryer, even one set on a cool temperature. People do not always realize that the tumbling action would cause severe felting, even without heat.

A printed slip of hints for using handspun yarn, such as we enclose with knitting yarn orders, can be a help to customers who have not previously used handspun. They may not otherwise know that they should not cut the yarn, but should break it, because the tapered end, left by breaking, weaves in well and will not pop out later. These hints also suggest that they join on a new ball by splicing it, knitting the first few inches along with the last few inches of the previous ball, with the yarn doubled for a few stitches. Since these are both tapered ends, the doubling is not noticeable. We also suggest that they not knit "blind," relying only on a stitch gauge and printed pattern. With handspun it is much safer to use a tape measure while knitting, checking the measurements of the garment against the desired finished measurements.

The more you can do to help customers, the more successful their first projects will be, so you will not only have happy customers, but also reorders.

Customer Correspondence

Keep customers' letters of inquiry on file for at least a few months, especially if they mention the type of article that they want to make with the yarn about which they are asking. If they do order the yarn later, they may not mention what they want to use it for, which is helpful information to know when you are spinning. Knitting and weaving requirements can differ. For example, a fine yarn for warp use will need a firmer twist than fine yarn for a knitted baby sweater, and even knitted socks will call for a different type of yarn than a knitted scarf.

It is not necessary to bother with making carbon copies of your replies; just note on their letters the date you answered and any special information you gave. If there was a price mentioned for a particular item, this should be noted, for by the time an order is placed, your price may have changed and you may have forgotten what price you had quoted.

Try to answer all letters as quickly as possible, not just for the sake of the customer, but also because, if letters start to pile up, it becomes depressing and makes them even harder to tackle. It saves time and postage to answer as fully as you can the first time, even trying to anticipate further ques-

Basket of handspun yarn. Skeins really show off the yarn best, but center-pull balls are convenient for knitting and crocheting. (By Priscilla Blosser-Rainey, Timberville, Virginia)

```
              WASHING INSTRUCTIONS

Articles made from this handspun yarn are very washable.
Use warm water and any mild soap or detergent, well
dissolved.  Rinse in water about the same temperature.
If unusual waterproof quality is desired, add about
1 Tbsp. clear salad oil to rinse water.  Sweaters dry
fast when water is spun out in spin-cycle of washer.
Small items can be rolled in towel, then laid out to
dry.  A light steam-pressing with wet cloth under iron
set at Wool temperature improves appearance.  Do not
dry in direct sunlight or in any type of clothes dryer.


    Handspun yarn by Paula Simmons, Suquamish, Wash.


    HANDSPUN by Paula Simmons
```

Good example of washing instructions, except that they really should say "hand washable."

tions. Their next letter to you may then be an order rather than a request for more information.

Promptness and Other Problems

Being prompt about filling orders is easier when you are just getting started and have fewer orders. Once you have a bulletin board of orders, enough to last for several weeks, and have perhaps given each customer an approximate delivery date, things get more complicated.

"First come, first served" sounds fair, but due to the nature of the orders, it is not always practical. An order that can be filled from wool that is already washed and carded invariably gets priority. One that requires considerably more preliminary work is easily put off. By the same token, if you have two orders for the same shade, it is simpler to do them at the same time, even though one of them may be more recent than some that are yet unfilled.

Ideally, it would be best to take only orders for yarn you have already made up, but that is not always possible. The next best thing would be to have the wool already carded up; the samples you send out would be from these carded colors that were ready for spinning. This can be done more easily if you have fleeces custom carded, in substantial quantities (see "Custom Carding Services" in "Sources" chapter). Unless you are spinning from a uniform source of white wool, none of these plans would help you

with an order from a customer who has kept your samples for a year or two before ordering.

Matching a color requested by a customer can be next to impossible unless you have the actual fleece or dye lot from which the sample was spun. We find that our customers are quite agreeable if we make it clear that we can only *approximate* the colors on our sample cards. We ask that they give second and even third choices in the event that we are not able to come close enough to their first selection with the wool that we have.

You will need some method, such as a bulletin board, for keeping track of orders. We attach the customer's letter, with yarn choices stapled to it, to the board. If the letter does not have a date in plain sight, we date it and record on it in large letters "Paid" or "Not paid." That way we do not have to go back in our receipt book to see if a payment has been made.

It is a good practice to acknowledge all orders received by mail; sending a postcard is sufficient. This is doubly important if the payment is sent with the order, so the customer will know it has arrived. Give an estimated delivery time, even though this was stated on your sample card; people do not always read and remember every word.

Even with the best of intentions, delivery dates are hard to keep when your bulletin board gets crowded and you try to squeeze in a few "rush" orders. We find that our weakness is putting off the orders from people who say "No hurry, whenever you have time." With no special deadline or

This note is printed on heavy paper and can be sent as a postcard to notify of the delivery date or can be enclosed in the package when it is sent. The "sorry sheep" illustration softens the message. (Paula Simmons)

promised delivery date, they get postponed from month to month.

Photographs and Labels

The person who is interested enough to buy is usually interested in the whole process. Enclosing a sheep photo, if you raise sheep, can show the customer the "source" of what they are buying. A photograph of you at your spinning wheel could serve the same purpose, if you do not have sheep.

Photos can be printed inexpensively by offset, but you must have extremely clear prints to work from if you want them to show up clearly; this method of printing causes some loss of detail.

Printers will "screen" photos for a small additional charge, and once they have been screened (reduced to a pattern of tiny dots) they will reproduce more clearly. Two five by seven-inch prints could be done on eight and one-half by eleven-inch glossy stock, and would be almost as satisfactory as photographic prints, at a fraction of the cost if you order by the hundred.

Another personal touch is a woven label. While you can get cloth labels in fabric shops, with first names already woven into them, they usually say "Handmade" or "Hand Sewn" rather than specifically "Handspun." You also can order small quantities of woven labels that have your name stamped or printed on them. Most knitting magazines have advertisements for these. While they are fine when giving yarn or garments to friends, they do not present a professional appearance to a handspun and handwoven garment that has to sell for a good price in order to justify the time and work it entails.

A number of large companies make woven labels to order, with the customer's choice of lettering and colors. These are designed to look expensive. The actual price per label would depend greatly on the quantity ordered, and some manufacturers have a minimum quantity they will make. A woven label saying "Handspun" and having your name on it could be sent with each order for a sweater quantity of yarn, and sewn into any garment that you weave, knit, or crochet for sale. The "Yellow Pages" in any large city's telephone directory list label manufacturers under "Labels, cloth" or "Labels, woven." (Refer also to "Sources" chapter.)

Gift Wrapping

Gift wrapping and mailing is a service you may want to offer at Christmastime. It can be indicated by a listing on your standard price list, either right after the price for small items that would be natural purchases for gifts, or added at the end of your price list as applying to all of your products—for example, "Gift wrapping $1 extra." This can pose a problem unless you can obtain a wrapping paper that is suitable, or have one designed for the purpose, and silk-screened or block printed. We started out with a silk-screened brochure to give out at a fair, and over a period of time the design used on it was adapted to stationery and to copyrighted wrapping paper. If you want to copyright a design, obtain all the information before you have the printing done. Request Form VA from the United States Copyright Office, Washington, D.C. 20559.

If you do offer gift wrapping and mailing on certain items, you will need to have them made up in advance and ready to mail immediately. Orders may come in for them when Christmas is only a few days away, as at that time it would be quite an advantage to a customer to be able to send you a gift card and have you mail the present for them.

Credit and Bad Checks

A certain amount of trust must exist between buyers and sellers. If customers send checks in advance, they must trust you to produce the yarn for them. If you spin the yarn and send it to them before they pay you, you trust that they will pay. We have not had any bills that have had to be written off as bad debts, and I have always gone on the assumption that people who like handspun just are not crooks.

Although we have received a few checks that bounced, it was not because the customers were trying to defraud us; they just accidentally overdrew their accounts, and sent us a replacement check the minute they found out about it. Maybe we have been awfully lucky.

In giving advice to someone else, I would have to say "exercise reasonable caution, particularly when large sums of money are involved."

Insurance

A shipment, whether paid in advance or not, is safer when insured. It need not necessarily be insured for full value, but do not insure it for the minimum amount either, for with minimum insured value, no one needs to sign for it at the other end. Insure large parcels for enough value that the customers, whether they are shops or individuals, will be required to sign for them. Even small packages may need insurance if you are sending them to a large city, especially to an apartment house address.

This copyrighted, hand silk-screened wrapping paper is a black design on manila paper. (Ross and Paula Simmons)

Advertising and Publicity

Advertising in some form is necessary. A relatively expensive item may justify a relatively expensive ad, but in most instances the less expensive the ad, the more frequently you can repeat it and the less crucial the outcome.

The most effective form of advertising is to be "discovered." Articles describing your lifestyle and method of working are particularly good publicity, because they call attention to your work without openly soliciting sales. What you are selling is what you do, and to the public, you and what you do are inseparable. Therefore, anything that is written about you is an advertisement for what you sell.

What is needed is to establish your name, associated with what you produce, in the mind of the public.

Newspapers

Since newspapers cannot stay in business without news to print, they work hard at finding a variety of things to write about in addition to usual calamities and politics. Besides what is written by their staff writers, they are usually receptive to free-lance articles, especially human interest stories that can be inserted whenever the newspaper needs something to fill out a half page or to help pad out the Sunday edition. Such stories need black-and-white photos, and if the writer gets good photographs, the article and its illustrations sometimes can be allotted a whole page. When you are the subject of such an article, the writer normally will see that you get copies of the photos; you also can get extra copies of the newspaper article for use in future publicity.

It seldom happens, but it helps considerably if you get to check an article for accuracy before the writer sends it in. Having no working knowledge of sheep, wool, and spinning, the writer and/or newspaper editor may get the details confused, or get them correct and then draw some strange conclusion. One example comes to mind. My husband had mentioned to a reporter that on a nice day he would shear three sheep and then come home to put the fleeces to soak, because a good day for shearing was also a good day for wool washing. The article related that on a good day my husband would shear as many as three sheep! That would get a snicker from anyone who knew much about sheep or shearing. Most articles have at least one "funny" thing in them, but it is nothing to get upset about. You can be fairly sure that most people do not read them carefully enough to notice.

I wish I could tell you a magic formula for being "discovered" and featured in articles, but I cannot. What will help is to be agreeable and cooperative, participate in craft events where you will be visible, and talk about what you are doing, especially the more unusual aspects of your work.

Once you get established, this will not pose a problem, for publicity tends to become self-perpetuating. Because you have been in the newspaper, someone else will hear about you and decide you are a good subject for an article of their own in a dif-

Sample of clear photo that could be sent with a press release. It shows several scarves being woven at one time, using handspun warp and weft. (Paula Simmons)

ferent paper or magazine.

In addition to the people who seek you out in order to write about "someone interesting doing something unusual," there may be other occasions when you are doing something of *particular* interest. This should be written up in detail and sent to the newspapers in the area.

Press Releases

Written announcements sent to newspapers are called "press releases" if they deal with a specific topic, such as an exhibit or a demonstration, the release of a book, or the organizing of classes. Press releases can get you free advertising, and make the most of all your public appearances, whether you are teaching, demonstrating, or just taking part in a craft show. In some instances, the only real value you will get out of an appearance is some good publicity.

If the sponsoring group, shop, or institution does not have an obviously capable publicity person, then take over and handle your own publicity. The customary procedure is for you to give them the details that they need, but in some cases you will be the only one who could get the facts straight, so it is best that you do write it (with their permission). Type the releases on their letterheads and envelopes rather than making it be too obvious that you are publicizing yourself.

Any notices and news releases sent to newspapers, magazines, television, or radio *must* be typed (double-spaced), as accurately and neatly as possible and on only one side of the paper. Include a release date on which, or after which, the information could be published, or indicate that it is "for immediate release."

In the first paragraph, give all the important information, such as who you are, what you are demonstrating or teaching (this should all be phrased in the third person), where it happens, the exact time and date, and for what occasion. *Then* elaborate on it, with a human interest angle if possible. Send along an eight by ten-inch black-and-white glossy photo if you can. Your name and address should be on a slip of paper taped to the back of the photo or written along the margin on the back, with a request to "return photo to..." Never send an irreplaceable photo, one for which you do not have duplicates or a negative, as there is always a possibility that it will be lost in the shuffle and not get mailed back.

If you do anything unusual in the production of your yarn or other items, mention it in the release—for example, if your whole family is involved in the activity; you raise your own sheep; you have unusual equipment, such as handmade processing tools of any kind or a spinning wheel that is unusual in appearance or origin; you use vegetable dyes made from local plants. If you conduct regular classes or give lessons in your home or studio, or if you are a member of a selling cooperative, or are connected in any way with a nonprofit shop or organization, include such information, also.

List any honors, awards, or recent gallery exhibits that would lend prestige to your work. Remember to keep it all written in the third person, so that the whole article sounds impersonal. Include a phone number where they could call to get additional information.

Newspapers do not like human interest or "art happening" stories to be blatantly commercial in case their paying advertisers would think that the paper is giving free advertising to your business. Consequently, some papers will not want to mention, directly, the selling aspect of your work. But you can imply it in a variety of ways without outright commercialism. Using a term such as "cottage industry," for example, is more acceptable than "business" or "shop."

Be sure to send releases to more than one newspaper. If you are sending to two large newspapers in the same city, try to phrase the release differently for each of them and send different photos. Also send releases to all the daily and weekly newspapers in the surrounding area. For weekly papers, find out what day they publish and mail the release so it arrives at their offices at least eight days ahead. Mail releases to magazines months ahead.

It is not too difficult to get press or media attention if what is written sounds interesting and "newsworthy."

Television

Television appearances seldom result in any direct sales; even if viewers are interested, they do not have time to find a pencil to write down your name and address. However, you can use these appearances to "build your image." When people have seen you once on television, they remember it when they see an article about you in a newspaper or magazine; the second exposure could produce results. A television appearance also could cause previous customers to contact you with an order.

Television will reach people who might not be particularly interested if they merely read something about you. Seeing you, especially in the activity of spinning or weaving, and hearing what you have to say about what you do and how you do it, can be more interesting. It still is not likely that they would rush out and buy your yarn, but when they do see you at a craft fair or see your yarn for sale in a shop, they might then be more apt to buy.

In most parts of the country, people have been sufficiently exposed to spinning in recent years that it may take more than sitting at a spinning wheel to keep their attention. Be sure viewers get something out of what you say, such as ideas about how they could use handspun yarn in knitting, crocheting, or weaving. Tell what they could make from it—not just a knitted sweater, but perhaps a pillow that is easy to make, using a technique such as hooking or crocheting. Tell how they could wear one of the garments you make, for a new high-fashion look, or the same garment layered for a casual and comfortable style. Tell them a bit about how to determine good craftsmanship in spinning or weaving, or how to care for

Our booth at a travel show in 1960. In return for free space and a cedar sheep pen, I demonstrated for ten hours each day for ten days, with a half hour for lunch each day while they had the ostrich races. It was my first experience with demonstrating; the advertising was good, the sales were very poor.

handspun, or how to protect garments from moths. Such useful information will make them glad they saw you and more likely to remember what they saw.

So how do you get on television programs? One way is to volunteer. Anytime you are going to be in a craft fair or some other publicized event, tell the publicity chairman that you would be available for television shows to advertise it. Mention that you could take your spinning wheel or wheels for demonstrating. It may sound like a lot of bother to take more than one wheel, but two distinct styles of wheels will add interest to the interview. Having these there can even result in more time being given to you on the air, since there will be more things

to talk about than the event being promoted, and your part in it.

When you are on the program, be sure to give all the facts. If you are talking about a craft fair, for example, tell the date and time, how many years it has been held, the number of people who usually attend, and how many years you have participated, if it has been for several years. These facts will need to be obtained ahead of time and memorized.

If there is an educational channel near you, offer to present a program about handspinning, including carding and spinning, and finish up by showing baskets of your yarn, explaining about yarn sizes and twist, plying and overtwist, and fancy textured

Small gift and supply shop connected with a craft school. The students may place their work for sale here, with a ten percent commission taken by the shop. Their special Christmas open house generates sales of student work. (Damascus School for Pioneer Crafts, Clackamas, Oregon)

yarns. Also show any woven or knitted items made by yourself or some of your yarn customers or any other examples of your finished work. Explain the superiority and uniqueness of handspun in relation to factory yarns, and focus on your own specialty and what makes it a little different.

Mailing List

Building up a card file of persons that you know are actually interested in your yarn can be a real asset. Include all customers, especially from craft fairs where you have so many contacts, and also people who write to inquire about your work, even if they do not purchase right then.

This list can be kept current by making one mailing a year, if it is sent first class. With your return address on the envelope, it will be returned to you if the customer has moved, and you can then take that name off your list. A price list or announcement of a new item, especially one that would make a good gift, could be sent out in time for Christmas orders; an offer to gift wrap and mail could be included in the price list. (Refer to the "Pricing" and "Selling" chapters for detailed information about price lists, catalogs, and sample cards, as well as mail-order selling.)

An open house at your studio is another occasion for sending out a mailing. Display an array of yarn and finished items, all priced. Serve coffee and tea, and show people around your studio, explaining processes and equipment. You will need at least one helper to write up sales while you are showing visitors around.

A newspaper ad, as distinct from a direct mailing, could be seen by many more people, but it would not necessarily reach the ones who are interested in you and what you are selling. It is the *personal* interest that produces the most results.

In the event of a gallery exhibit, have announcements or invitations (usually provided by the gallery) sent to the customers on your list. You may reason that you would prefer they buy direct from you, rather than sending proven customers to a gallery to buy. However, the announcement can be more in the way of advertising for you than for the gallery. It is unlikely that many of your customers, especially those from any distance away, will actually attend the exhibit. What you are doing is just telling them you have been honored with an exhibit, which reminds them that you are still in business. The result can be a purchase made directly from you at that time or even long after the exhibit is over.

Educational Exhibits

There are often occasions for "educational exhibits" where you are asked to demonstrate spinning or show some of your work, or both, but are not allowed to sell because of the nature of the sponsoring organization—for instance, a library, school, or nonprofit club. Look on these affairs as a way to let the buying public know what you are doing. Pass out price lists or brochures, and make it plain that you are in business, even if you cannot make sales during the event. Ask the sponsor if press releases have been sent out. If not, offer to do it or to assist in sending them.

Demonstrations are often sought for county fairs or livestock exhibits, in connection with sheep and/or wool. When asked to demonstrate under these circumstances, you could quote a fee and then suggest you would rather take it out in clean, skirted fleeces. Take your price lists and brochures to hand out, and have with you a large basket of your yarn—all washed, blocked, and labeled.

Considering the money and time spent in assembling materials, traveling, and demonstrating, it is not unreasonable to expect a fee. In many parts of the country, spinners always get paid for demonstrating, but in other places no one has been bold enough to mention money, so everyone is still doing it for free. If spinning groups would discuss this and agree that a fee is proper, it would not take long to make "paid demonstrations" an accepted practice everywhere. It would seem that at least the minimum wage per hour would be a reasonable request, and would not be such a large sum as to be financially unfeasible for the sponsor.

Spinners who have a printed price list can save themselves the awkwardness of having to break the news that they charge if they put on their price list "Demonstration fee on request." This does not mean that they cannot quote a fee and then bargain instead for a certain type of publicity (advertising).

One time you would not want to charge is when the demonstration is for a shop that sells your yarns. In this instance, you may suggest that they advertise your presentation, either in the newspaper or by a special mailing to their customers. It is to their advantage to advertise it in some way, and it is to your advantage to draw attention to the fact that they stock your yarn, and cooperate in the publicizing of it.

When you are asked to set up an exhibit of your work to be left up for several weeks, and you will not be there demonstrating or handing out price lists, it is especially important that you have labels and tags in clear view. Libraries, for instance, have large glass display cases, in which they have different exhibits every week or two. An array of yarn and a variety of handspun items, including some wool in various stages of processing, is one possibility for a display. The library ordinarily will supply cards with captions on them for the different parts of the display. Good clear photographs of anything connected with your work are also interesting, and a valuable part of the promotion. If this kind of exhibit sounds like something you would like to do, just assemble a collection of your work and some photos, then make the rounds of all the libraries within convenient driving distance.

Other Exposure

Anyplace your yarn or products, with your name attached to them, are seen will constitute good exposure when you are trying to let the public know you are in business. For example, an arts and crafts auction to benefit a nonprofit museum or shop can be a form of advertising for you. There are two ways it might be handled. Those running the auction can ask for a donation of merchandise, with all proceeds going to the sponsoring organization. Or they can ask for merchandise to auction, with a commission (such as forty or fifty percent) going to the "worthy cause" and the rest going to the craftsman.

If you have enough time to tackle a large project, you might organize a craft auction as a fund-raising project for a local charity. This would result in publicity for your own work as well as that of other craftsmen.

Exposure of a completely different kind

Work of the Xochi Spinners Co-op displayed in weaving shop window. (Straw into Gold, Oakland, California)

would be a juried craft exhibit, which may require things you do not normally do. If you want to enter, take a cold-blooded look at the kind of thing that would most likely get in and produce accordingly. While "fiber art" pieces are not always as salable as functional items, they do provide good publicity if accepted in a show. You hear it said that entries have to be either very good or very gaudy, but it is understandable that in order to be successful, a show needs pieces that are both well crafted and spectacular. Anything intended for a juried exhibit should be impressive, yet extremely well done.

For shows in other areas of the country, you will have to weigh the cost of entry and shipping against the possibility of not getting in.

Labels and Tags

The labels or tags that you put on your yarn and other items can constitute effective advertising for you wherever they are sold, and they continue to advertise even after they have been purchased.

The tags or bands on yarn skeins should have your name on them, and a recognizable logo. For selling in shops, the tags should not have your address on them, because the shop does not want to encourage customers to order directly from you. Actually, customers would often rather buy from the shop, for there they can choose from an array of shades and different skein weights, and have immediate delivery instead of waiting for their order to be spun.

Since in a shop your yarn will have direct competition from factory-spun yarns, many of them a "homespun type" that is made to resemble handspun, it is important for your tag to convey that your yarn actually *is* handspun. Having your name on the label, as the spinner of the yarn, is one way to emphasize this fact. Some spinners also tell the name of the sheep. We did that at one time, but found it caused complications. Customers would want the wool of the same sheep the next year, not understanding that dark sheep are usually a shade lighter each year, or at least not exactly the same color.

Labels and tags should look professional, but not commercial; they should reflect the feeling of a handmade product. Hand silk-screening or block printing would be a good family project for turning out a supply of labels. A large investment is not even needed to provide a good variety of coordinated tags and labels that are commercially printed. Drawn on white paper with black ink, they can be reproduced by offset printing on whatever weight and color of paper you choose. They can be lettered and drawn on a single sheet of eight and one-half by eleven-inch paper (the cheapest size to reproduce) that is divided up to make several different tags, a yarn skein band or two, and one strip the width of the paper for printing yarn-washing instructions. When printed by the hundreds, the cost is very little. The pages can be cut up to make separate tags and labels. Most printers charge extra for each cut they make, such as fifty cents per cut with a minimum cutting charge of two

dollars. If several hundred printed pages need to be cut into tags and labels, it is worthwhile to have the printer make the cuts, nice and square and neat. This takes only a few minutes, as their cutter will slice through hundreds of pages at one time.

In some instances a label or tag could be registered as a trademark. This is done through the United States Patent Office, Washington, D.C. 20231. A booklet called *General Information Concerning Trademarks* is available for fifty cents from the United States Government Printing Office, Washington, D.C. 20402.

Gummed address labels are inexpensive and can be used for bands on tiny skeins, such as stitchery, embroidery, or needlepoint skeins. These labels can be ordered with up to four lines of printing (no more than twenty-four letters and spaces per line), and cost about one dollar for a thousand labels. By including the shop name on them, you can get a personalized set of labels for each shop that sells your small skeins. We wrap a label around each skein (or around part of the skein), lap the ends over each other, and fasten them with Scotch Brand Magic Transparent Tape, which is almost invisible on the labels and attaches them more securely than the glue on the labels does.

Advertising

There is a limit to the amount of yarn that can be produced by one person, even a fast spinner; expensive advertising may not

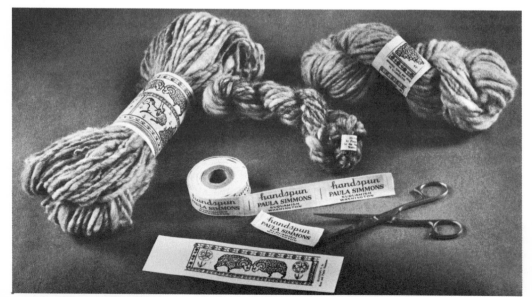

Three ways of labeling skeins— band around a folded skein, band around a portion of a twisted skein, and tiny address-label band around the end of a small tapestry skein. In the foreground is a silk-screened paper label (also for use on a skein of yarn) with "belligerent ram" logo. In the center is a part of a roll of woven labels with black lettering on pale gray.

be warranted when the cost could not be offset by an immense volume of sales. Without volume, the money you spend on advertising increases the amount of your overhead costs, and results either in having higher prices on your merchandise or a smaller profit margin.

Actual paid advertising should be done selectively so you can get the most possible sales per dollar spent. You could use the classified section, which is cheaper than space-by-the-inch, in spinning or weaving magazines, or try magazines that cater to an audience other than persons specifically interested in fibers and yarns. Classified ads in neighborhood or city newspapers will reach people within driving distance of your studio.

An ad for handspun should suggest uniqueness and exclusiveness, and focus on your specialty. Keep the ad simple, and appeal to a customer's discernment. Options for advertising include: (1) advertising yarn, and offering a sample card for one or two dollars; (2) advertising a small article that can be produced easily, requiring only a small amount of yarn and little time to make, and having high-volume potential; and (3) advertising a large and more expensive article, such as a coat or couch throw, which would result in fewer sales but more profit per sale.

A few kinds of advertising that require a small initial investment can continue indefinitely to work for you. Such advertising includes a bumper sticker, a small poster that can be left on bulletin boards or public-service reader boards, and a sign for your gate, door, or auto.

Long-Term Advertising

Advertising is not intended to give only *immediate* results; part of its value is in building an image. It is not always the importance of each occasion that you should look at, but the total and cumulative effect. I have heard craftsmen complain about how poor the sales were at a particular fair, then hear a few weeks later that, because of the fair, they have landed a big wholesale order that will keep them busy for months. You never know what contact may occur at a seemingly unimportant event.

A lot of the cumulative value of advertising is lost, however, if you change your address. If possible, stay put. When you stay in

the same place, doing the same thing, you build up a following of customers who know where you are and have confidence in you as a serious craftsman. They also like to think that if they have a problem with your merchandise, you will still be in the same place and will stand behind your work. Moving somehow sounds unstable, and anything that even suggests unreliability will tend to discourage customers from sending you money for yarn not yet received. This does not mean that if you move, you cannot succeed; it just means that moving around is a real disadvantage.

Business sign on the porch of a home-studio. (Sachiye Jones, Eugene, Oregon)

Related Income

Earning a living with handspun yarn alone can mean hours and hours of spinning for days on end. Articles made up from your own yarn result not only in considerably more money for the yarn that is used, but also afford a more varied kind of activity. There is also the need to encourage the use of handspun by exemplifying its distinctive qualities when put to its best possible use. How effectively you use it yourself can encourage and inspire others in the uses of handspun, which will in turn create an even greater demand for your product. Added to this will be the satisfaction of fully utilizing the inherent qualities of a particular fleece and a particular shade, which only the spinner can fully appreciate. With the finished product, you have the sense of having completely explored its usefulness as yarn.

By the same token, teaching and writing answer the need to explore the possibilities of the yarn-making process. Teaching requires a sharpened awareness of the other person's problems and what proficiency is all about. When writing, the need is to present as clearly as possible whatever hard and useful information you have in a way that is both clarifying and challenging. Being able to do it yourself is not enough. We are in full possession of only those things that we can impart to others.

Weaving

One of the more effective ways of using handspun yarn is in weaving. Some spinners were already weavers when they started spinning, but all spinners should gain a practical knowledge of weaving if they intend to sell their yarn to weavers. Weaving with handspun presents a few problems not always encountered when using factory-spun yarn. These problems vary with different types of handspun, and should be explained to customers.

In weaving with your own yarn, the challenge is to come up with a salable item. The simplest solution would appear to be the weaving of yardage, but in most areas, yardage is the hardest product to sell. Unless you can tie in with someone who will have it tailored for their own customers, you may have to do the sewing in order to sell it. A few shops and galleries buy handwoven yardage and have it tailored into clothing they can sell in their own shop, but this is unusual. Most prefer the finished product. If yardage is what you would like to do, assemble folios of samples and contact dressmakers to find a few who would keep your samples on hand to show to their customers. They would want to mark up the price per yard when showing the samples, so your price should not appear on the sample folders.

Pillows can be made from handspun yardage and sold at craft fairs or to shops. The main problem here is the concealed stuffing laws that exist in most states. These require a license or permit, usually for a high fee, in order to make and sell stuffed items such as pillows and comforters. It is not always enforced in all states, but there have been incidents when inspectors have

Woven yardage with matching sweater yarn, shown in a gallery exhibit. (Handspun by Paula Simmons; weaving by Lewis Mayhew, Seattle, Washington)

stopped the sale of pillows at craft fairs. One way to get by this is to buy an inner pillow with the permit declaration attached to it, and sew this inside your woven cover, leaving a few inches on the edge unsewn so the declaration can be seen. We make a few pillows for the one craft fair we work, and I am prepared to insist that "those stuffed things" are oversized pincushions.

We never plan ahead to weave pillows, but if we have a short length of warp left over, not enough to make a coat or vest, we weave it up as pillow fabric. Other times an article, such as a stole, that did not sell readily is recycled into several pillows. We frequently make more on the pillows than we would have made on the stole.

Another yardage-type project is the weaving of afghans or couch throws, which need no finishing other than knotting of the fringes and washing. When made with smaller dimensions, they can be sold as baby blankets, ponchos, or lap robes. By dividing the width of the warp and weaving with two shuttles and four selvedges, you could make stoles. By dividing the width of the warp into three or four sections, three or four scarves can be made at once.

When making garments for sale, the tailoring can be simplified by doing whatever loom shaping will make the finishing of seams easier or less bulky. We have found the most salable items are those that are unfitted, such as sleeveless vests or loose coats, which we make in only two sizes (the size being determined by the width of the loom used).

One decision related to weaving is whether or not to use your handspun for warp. In any weft-faced weaving, such as in tapestries or saddle blankets where the warp is not even seen, it would be a waste of time and wool to spin the warp, so sturdy cotton or linen warp is generally used.

Some spinners use commercial warps because the price they can get for the article does not warrant spinning both warp and weft. Yet when it comes to price, many of the good commercial warp yarns are not that much cheaper than handspun, so the prime concern could still be the time it takes to spin suitable warp yarn.

We use our own handspun (singles) for all our warps, treating the chains with sizing to prevent any weaving problems. When using natural-colored handspun in a wide range of shades, we would not want to be limited to the relatively narrow selection of natural shades that can be purchased in homespun-type warp yarn. Those who use vegetable dyes can dye a homespun-type yarn to go with their dyed handspun wefts, and not have difficulty with color coordination. In our own case, we actually prefer to spin our own warp. There is a satisfaction in knowing that, for good or ill, the end result is completely our own product.

Unspun Wool

All wool is not equally suited for hand-spinning. A fleece that has a lot of second cuts and small seeds requires more hand-work than it warrants. Rather than spending hours trying to salvage such wool for spinning, it is better to find a more suitable use for it.

Unspun Wool in Rugs

Fleece rugs made from uncarded and unspun wool woven on heavy linen or wool warp can tie in well with your other products. These rugs are most durable when made from a long, coarse type of wool, such as Lincoln, Cotswold, or Karakul. (We call them "Richard rugs" because for a number of years we used the fleece from our Lincoln ram, named Richard, for weaving fleece rugs.) Even a matted fleece can be used if it can be pulled apart in small enough locks. The fleece can be laid into a broken-twill shed, using enough tufts or locks to form a

Pillows of handspun yarn. The round pillow is crocheted of medium weight singles, the rectangular pillow is woven with a border of sumac and rya knots. (By Priscilla Blosser-Rainey, Timberville, Virginia)

Mid-sleeve shepherd coat, hip-length sleeveless vest, and long sleeveless coat, all woven of natural colored handspun. (By Ross and Paula Simmons)

weft, and beaten in tightly. Then a binder yarn can be thrown across in a tabby shed, and another broken twill shed opened for another laid-in section of fleece. The finished effect depends much on the kind of fleece and its condition. The use of different natural shades, either random or patterned, can make rugs more attractive.

Unspun Wool in Hooking

Unspun wool can be used for hooking, either by itself or in combination with odds and ends of warp thrums. Carded wool, separated into strips, can be hooked through rug canvas (holding the wool under the canvas and pulling loops up through the canvas) to make thick rugs. Saddle blankets can be made by hooking on burlap.

Preshrunk burlap could also be cut into a garment shape, and hooked with carded wool strips. Hook almost out to the seam allowance, then sew the garment pieces together and finish up the hooking in the sections next to the seams. For the fronts of a jacket, fold back the raw edges of burlap and hook the wool through both thicknesses to make a nicely finished edge. This same

method would be used for the hem at the bottom of a jacket and at the cuff edges.

Unspun Wool in Felting

Fleeces that cannot be used for spinning without spending an unreasonable amount of time on them can be used instead for felting, with some extremely salable results. By using up whatever is available, you eliminate waste and save money. (See "Sources" chapter for literature about felting.)

I was quite inspired by dyed felt mittens made by Pat Boutin Wald and a luxurious coat made by Louise Green of Greentree Ranch. Then one year when I taught in Bandon, Oregon, I went down a day early to sit in on a felting workshop. I was surprised to see the thick amount of wool used, and how it was compressed and felted into a pad that was such a small fraction of the thickness of the original layered wool. The outer layer of wool used is all that is seen; the wool in between can be the kind that is ordinarily thrown away.

Felting can be done with washed wool or grease wool, but it is easier to make the layers of an even thickness if the wool has

Small box of stitchery yarn in assorted colors. (By Paula Simmons)

been carded—either hand carded, drum carded, or custom carded. I know of one shop owner who skirts all her fleeces before selling them, and saves the skirtings until she has one hundred pounds. Then she bundles it all up and sends it off for scouring and custom carding. The carded wool is sold for felting.

The surface design possibilities are almost limitless. Yarn patterns can be laid onto the layered wool before it is felted, or areas of dyed wool can be surface embellishments. The finished felt can be soft or firm, smooth or pebbled, depending on the technique.

In addition to mittens and coats, after-ski boots can be made, as well as hats (shaped over bowls as they are being felted), and cushions or seat covers or clothing (made from flat pieces).

Dyeing

The idea of doing handspun vegetable dyed yarn is hard to resist. However, the cost of purchasing the necessary indigo and cochineal, plus the time needed to gather dye plants for the rest of the color range, makes it difficult to price the yarn so that it is both salable and profitable. It is also hard to gather sufficient dye materials to produce good color in large amounts of wool or yarn.

One way to get a fair price for plant dyed handspun is to dye it in large quantities, but package it in very small quantities, such as a tiny box of assorted colors. We did dyeing at one time, and found that boxes of six or eight skeins of various colors sold nicely, and at a price that was quite acceptable. Boxes sold even faster if we had only one color range per box.

In dyeing, as you exhaust your dye vat you get several shades of a color. By packaging a range of reds and pinks in one box, a selection of yellows and oranges in one box, green shades in another, and blues in another, the customer who would have purchased only one box of a range of colors would now purchase four boxes to get all the subtle shades. These packaged skeins were good for selling at craft fairs and wholesale to shops. The only drawbacks to marketing in that way were the cost of custom-made boxes with transparent lids, and the amount of time needed to wind all the little skeins, arrange them in boxes, and put labels on the boxes.

Instead of dyeing the yarn, we found it simpler to do all of our dyeing with washed fleeces. This ensured a uniformity of color after the wool was carded, and allowed the option of spinning the dyed wool into whatever yarn size we needed. Some of the pale and medium gray fleeces were very unusual when dyed.

We did take a shortcut: washing the wool and rinsing it well, then taking it directly from the rinse (after the water was spun out in our extractor) into the dye bath without premordanting. The mordants, a combination of alum and cream of tartar, were right in with the dye. I cannot say whether this method could be used as successfully with other mordants. These were the only mordants we ever used, partly because they are less toxic than others, such as chrome, and also do not pose a disposal problem.

While an "investigative" method is great for enjoying the pleasure of dyes and color, and fine for experiments, we find that in selling yarn, the use of some standard procedure will save much time. It need not be the most common method, but once you get things down to a system, it can be repeated easily without spending time making decisions.

If you are dyeing your wool in the fleece, this would also make it possible to use a custom carding service, which would blend wool so thoroughly that there would be no streakiness in the yarn. Wool that is to be custom carded would need less stirring in the dye bath, so that matting or snarling would be minimized.

In sending several colors of dyed wool (or natural colors, for that matter) out at one time for carding, be sure to label each bag to be carded separately. I had a friend who sent four shades to be carded, and the mill carded them all up together. It resulted in a beautiful heather color, but it was not what she had had in mind.

There is also a market for chemical dyed handspun. Here the emphasis is on the handspun aspect, and it is usually heavily textured. Some people spin from uncarded wool to obtain maximum texture, and then dye the yarn. Others dye the fleece before spinning, and do a minimum of carding. These unusual textured colors are popular with weavers. Since using chemical dyes eliminates the time needed to gather plants

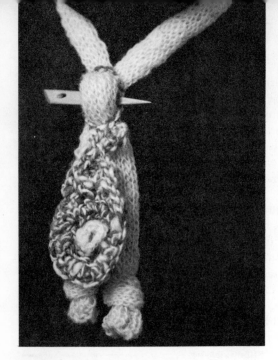

and makes it possible to repeat dye lots, it is easier to come out ahead when pricing it for sale.

The other way to go with dyeing is to use vegetable dyes on commercial "homespun-type" yarn. Some spinners have tried selling vegetable dyed handspun and found they could not make a fair wage, while by dyeing white mill yarn they were able to sell it profitably. Sheep-raising spinners who want to dye commercial yarn can send quantities of one hundred pounds (all will be carded into one color) to either Harrisville Designs or Bartlettyarns (see "Sources" chapter) and get their own wool back in homespun-type yarn for dyeing.

The best selling yarn for vegetable dyed mill yarn seems to be almost the opposite of the fastest selling handspun—a fine weight vegetable dyed yarn sold in small skeins sells well for needlepoint and crewel work. Since both of these uses require a smoothly spun yarn, the evenness of commercial yarn in this instance can be an asset.

There is one problem caused by vegetable dyed commercial yarn. In using homespun mill yarns, the dyer may have no intent to mislead, but can confuse the customer by labeling the yarn "Vegetable dyed homespun." The customer usually assumes that it is hand-dyed and hand-spun ("spun in someone's home"). Some shops do not discourage this assumption. If it were called "homespun-type," it would avoid confusion, and account for the difference in price that must be charged by spinners who are trying to sell actual handspun yarn, dyed with natural dyes.

Knitting and Crocheting

One real advantage knitting and crocheting have over weaving is that you can take your work with you. Small items such as socks, caps, or mittens can be taken wherever you go, and worked on in time that otherwise would be unproductive. These smaller articles do well at craft fairs. Besides being one of a kind and in a moderate price range, they are also useful, and whether or not they fit or are becoming can be decided easily.

A great many women knit or crochet, and if they choose they can buy the kind and amount of yarn to make whatever interests them. But as a rule, when they find something attractive they will buy it already made rather than buying yarn they may never get around to using.

Unlike weaving, crocheting and knitting do not require having pounds of finished yarn already spun before you begin. One skein and you are on your way, with quite a variety of small items that can be done with only a few ounces. More adventuresome knitting or crocheting can be done as free-form designing, where the garment is shaped and embellished as you go along, without following a set pattern or plan.

Since it takes so many hours to knit a sweater, some spinners who sell sweaters at fairs, or take custom orders for them, have one or more knitters working for them on a piecework basis. Others make the sweaters themselves, knitting in their spare time all year around in order to have them done up

Neckpiece knit of white, fine singles of Corriedale fleece, with crocheting in variegated gray and white yarn, and small crocheted circle of handspun mohair. (By Priscilla Blosser-Rainey, Timberville, Virginia)

Knitted ski headband with crocheted edging, made of handspun singles in brown and beige. (By Paula Simmons)

ahead for sale at fairs.

For selling at a craft fair, we find we have less of a fitting problem if we make up only sleeveless pullovers. They also take less time and yarn than a sweater with sleeves, and can be priced considerably lower.

Some spinners have specialties that are quite unique and easily identified as their work. For example, I have seen knitted and crocheted stuffed animals, some stunning knitted lace shawls and stoles, and soft jewelry and body ornaments, which are especially attractive when made from dyed yarns.

Stitchery and Needlepoint

Stitchery and needlepoint are two more ways of using handspun yarn to produce marketable products. Stitchery can get the absolute maximum effect from a given amount of yarn, as it can be done in stitches such as couching, outline, and Cretan stitch, where most of the yarn is right on the surface. And stitchery wall hangings can be done on different backgrounds for quite different appearances. Burlap or other loosely woven fabrics can allow one result, while silk organza or woven Swiss straw can produce an entirely different mood. Bayeaux stitch or satin stitch can produce a solid surface, entirely hiding whatever fabric is used.

Spinners will be partial to handspun yarn on handspun and handwoven fabric. Here infinite contrast can be produced by the many yarn sizes and textures, as well as the variety of natural wool shades, vegetable

"Saint George" stitchery done in natural colored handspun on handspun woven fabric. (Weaving by Paula Simmons; stitchery by Ann Meerkerk, Greenbank, Washington)

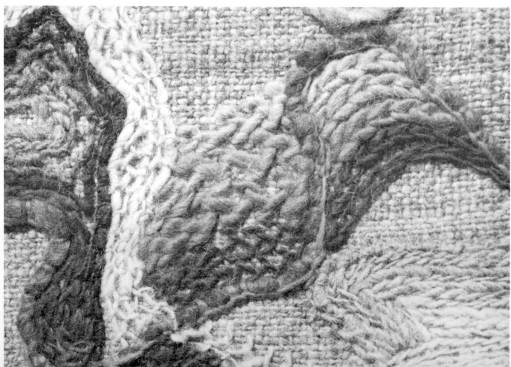

Detail of gray wool couch throw woven of natural colored handspun. Stitchery is all handspun, in couched yarns, outline Cretan, blanket, slant, chain stitch, and square chain. (Weaving and yarn by Paula Simmons; stitchery by Cleo Francisco, Seattle, Washington)

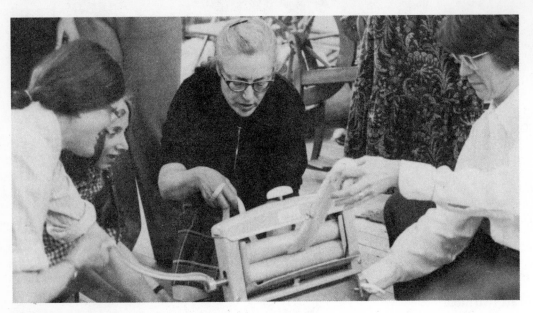

Temporary setup of hand wringer to demonstrate the sizing of warp chains for Minneapolis Weavers Guild. (Paula Simmons)

dyed colors, and variegated tweedy yarns.

Needlepoint is a technique that is adaptable to many sizes and shapes. Christmas ornaments and pincushions are two small items that are readily marketable and can be done with yarn leftovers. I have seen attractive hats and even vests done in needlepoint with heavy yarn.

Ambitious needlepoint and stitchery projects like custom-designed chair seats or upholstery can best be merchandised by working with an interior designer.

Teaching

It is not completely necessary to teach in order to make a living at spinning. I know this from other successful spinners as well as from my own experience. I did no teaching at all for the first eighteen years that we sold yarn. However, I do think that the majority of spinners who are trying to make their living at spinning are involved in some form of teaching.

There are several good reasons to include teaching in your overall plan for spinning-related income:

1. You can earn money without using up raw materials.
2. It gives you an occasion to sharpen your own skills in order to come up with a clear and communicable technique.
3. You can, through your teaching, help stimulate greater interest in hand-spinning and in the use of handspun yarn.

By far the most prevalent form of teaching is that of a series of classes, held once a week, usually for two to four hours. These are often held in spinning-weaving shops, and are either taught by the owner or by paid instructors. Classes usually result in the sale of supplies to the students. Having the classes does not require an added investment for inventory in order to have a larger shop income; therefore, the fees from classes can be a major factor keeping a small shop in business until there is an established following of customers.

In areas without spinning-weaving shops, classes can be held in the home-studio of the teacher, who usually will have some spinning equipment and supplies for sale. One large room, rather than two adjoining rooms, is preferable for teaching. Even if much of the class time is spent in giving individual attention to students, part of the benefit of classes is for each person to be able to hear what the teacher is saying to others.

Another type of class is a residential workshop or a semiresidential workshop with lodging arranged nearby. Examples of this are the summer workshops held for two weeks by Marilyn Jones in Kansas and the spinning and dyeing residential workshops at Edna Blackburn's Albion Hills Farm School in Ontario (see "Workshops" section in "Sources" chapter). These places both keep sheep, in addition to teaching spinning. For those who are also interested in sheep raising, this kind of arrangement has a definite advantage.

Hal Painter and Jim Brown have been

offering a series of two-week summer workshops in Chiloquin, Oregon. These are in a private campground beside a river, and the students bring tents and campers. Classes are held each morning, and the rest of the day is left for the students to enjoy the high desert location, go swimming, pick dye plants, or work on their tapestries. Hal teaches the tapestry weaving, using mostly handspun yarn, and Jim teaches vegetable dyeing. They bring in guest instructors for spinning or other crafts.

Most craft schools have occasional openings for new teachers, even if they have a paid staff with teachers instructing in their own special fields. The Damascus School for Pioneer Crafts in Oregon, which opened in April 1968, is a partnership of four working

instructors, but still hires outside teachers for some classes. They have fifteen assorted spinning wheels, a centrifugal extractor, and six drum carders in addition to looms and other equipment.

A person interested in teaching but not having adequate home space could contact local weaving shops that do not already have regular spinning classes. They may be contemplating classes but have no one in mind to conduct them.

In addition to that, get in touch with county and city parks and recreation facilities. In most parts of the country, they have regular craft classes with paid instructors. Jean Woodward of Hemlock Hill Handspinners in Maryland, teaches classes in her home studio, with students signed up by the

Craft school where students get instruction and experience on different types of looms. (Damascus School for Pioneer Crafts)

Old rural schoolhouse building renovated into a complete craft school facility. By having a variety of craft classes, there is always a good enrollment. (Damascus School for Pioneer Crafts, Clackamas, Oregon)

Instructor giving individual help to a spinning student. Spinners can bring their own wheels or use the ones belonging to the school. (Amy Miller, Damascus School for Pioneer Crafts)

park department.

Other places to apply would be the therapy section of hospitals, rest homes where crafts are taught for rehabilitation, museum schools, the YMCA and YWCA, and at army bases. The Peace Corps, which requires a two-year commitment, places teachers in foreign countries to set up cottage industry projects. While some of these places do not pay much, you will get experience and references, and can go on from there.

Writing

If you are enthusiastic and knowledgeable about what you do, then chances are that you could write successfully about it.

Since it is much easier to get a magazine article accepted for publication than it is to sell a book manuscript, consider that first. *Sunset, Yankee, Country Journal, Organic Gardening and Farming,* and *The Mother Earth News* are a few of the periodicals that do print craft articles, from time to time, and pay fairly well.

Newspapers are another market for selling articles. The large newspapers buy from free-lance writers, especially illustrated stories for their Sunday pictorial sections, which require very good black-and-white photographs. When newspapers buy a story, they pay for one-time use of the photos, so these can be used again to illustrate an article for a paper in a different part of the country. Potential subjects for such a project could be a local spin-in, a weaving or spinning booth at a craft fair, or a spinner's family involvement in sheep, including all the home processes.

The biggest market for spinning-related articles would be the smaller fiber magazines. They are usually on a tight budget and limited in what they can pay, but there is another way you can make money from your articles. While they are automatically copyrighted when they appear in the publication, you should ask ahead of time for permission to make and sell offset reprints of the articles. These would just be added to your price list. I am still selling reprints of eleven of the articles I wrote between 1962 and 1974 for *Handweaver & Craftsman* magazine, which went out of business in 1974. In aiming for a reprint income, you would need to write the type of articles that have reference value, with information that continues to be useful year after year. Aside from the possible reprint value, the articles themselves could be considered as the basis of a book, in which you could present the subject matter in greater detail.

Once you have had a few articles published in magazines, you will have some tangible evidence to send to a prospective book publisher to show that you are recognized as a writer in your field. This is important, for their staff will be competent to judge your writing ability, but are not likely to be familiar with the subject matter.

Before approaching a publisher, it will be time well spent if you go to the library and read through recent (annual) issues of *Literary Market Place, Writer's Market,* and *Writer's Handbook* as these books give a lot of information about what publishers are looking for in handcraft manuscripts, and also what publications are interested in free-lance articles. You will not want to waste a lot of postage and time by contacting the wrong markets.

The usual way to contact a publishing company is to send them an outline of the book, a sample chapter, and copies of one or more of the photos and drawings that will be used, keeping a copy of everything sent. In the letter that accompanies all this, give a listing of other books in the same field against which yours will compete. Tell them why you think another book is warranted and why it will sell. Stress what is unique and different about your book. Also send copies of the magazine articles you have written. In order to get your material back, you will have to enclose a large, stamped, self-addressed envelope. When you send a manuscript to a large publisher, it is ordinarily several months before you hear back from them as to whether they accept or reject it.

If your manuscript is accepted, you will be sent two copies of a contract, one to be signed and sent back and one for your files. Read the agreement carefully and do not be afraid to ask questions if any point is unclear. The contract will mention a title for your book, but it is written as "tentatively titled" and the publisher will have *complete* choice of the title and the cover design, unless the contract says otherwise. It will set a deadline for delivery of a "satisfactory manuscript" and will state the percentage of royalty that you will be paid for each book they sell. Some publishers pay a percentage of the retail price of the book, whether they sell it retail or wholesale. Others pay a percentage based on the actual price they get for each book, whether they sell it retail or wholesale or to book dealers who in turn sell it wholesale. The contract also will state that you get a certain number of free books (customarily twelve) at publication.

Most publishers offer a certain "advance," which is money paid to you in advance of the time you earn it. Whatever the amount of the advance, this is deducted from the royalty they will owe you from sales of the book. As a rule, they have a formula by which they determine how much of an advance they will offer. This could be based on the amount of royalty they think they will owe you for the first six months' sales. The purpose of the advance is to provide authors with money to live on while they are devoting all their time to finishing a book. The amount of time you would be working on a book will probably be time off from spinning and weaving. The year I wrote a sheep-raising book, our wholesale yarn income was down $2,000.

The contract will spell out what other conditions will affect the income you get from the book. For example, the contract usually states that the author will get no royalty on remainders, which are the overstock of books that may not be selling fast enough, if the publisher decides to sell them at remainder prices (usually a discount of seventy-five percent). If the publisher allows the book to go out of print for as long as six months, the author is commonly allowed to purchase the plates of the book at a certain fraction of their original cost.

In all contracts, to my knowledge, the publisher decides the selling price, the title, the cover design, and the style of the book. Some contracts give the publisher the first option on the next book written by the author, and most contracts forbid the author to publish a similar book that would interfere with the sale of the book specified in the contract.

This may sound like the publisher is calling all the shots, and so they are. But they are investing a lot of money in the book, not just in the typesetting and printing, but also in the time their staff spends in the editing, designing, advertising, and the sending out of press releases and review copies. They want to do everything possible to make their investment pay off.

In addition to regular book publishers, there are some that specialize in craft books, usually paperback booklets with color photographs. Some of these are how-to books about various crafts, and some are books showing specific projects in certain crafts, such as macrame, and have instructions, drawings, and color photos. In most instances, the books are written by the publisher's paid staff, who scout the craft fairs looking for specific pieces that they can feature in their project books. When they find something unusual, they buy a sample of it and offer the craftsman a fee to supply the directions for making it. They also buy projects from free-lance writers. These publishers seldom pay a royalty, but instead make a lump-sum payment for the material.

Self-Publishing

If you are unable to find a publisher for your manuscript and you feel sure that it would sell if you could only get it in print, then you should consider self-publishing. By this I do not necessarily mean going to a "vanity press," which charges you for editing, typesetting, publishing, binding, and promoting your book. Some of their advice may be helpful, such as telling you what price you will have to charge in order to make money, whether the photos you have will reproduce well, and how many books you will have to sell just to break even. But you will probably be paying out quite a bit more than if you made all the arrangements

yourself, and had it typeset, printed, and bound in your own area. By working closely with the printer, you can have complete control over the type style, size, format, cover, and title.

In deciding the price to charge for a book that you are having privately printed, be sure to allow for a wholesale price that will still give you a margin of profit. While you might sell a certain amount of books by advertising in spinning and weaving magazines, the bulk of your sales may be to shops, and they will expect the usual forty percent book discount.

One example of self-publishing is Frederick Gerber's book *Indigo and the Antiquity of Dyeing*. When his manuscript was rejected as being "too technical," he had it set in typeset and printed. It has enjoyed good sales and very favorable reviews.

One possibility for printing booklets and small books is having them printed by offset from typed pages. This is what I did with my *Patterns for Handspun*. The pattern directions were typed out and the photos pasted in place. (It costs a little more to have it done offset if you are using photos; drawings are easier and less expensive to reproduce.) The offset printer reduced the size just enough so that the typed instructions looked more like they were typeset. A typed book does not have as professional an appearance, but it can be done for a much smaller investment and so can be sold at a lower price.

A self-published book that has very good sales can sometimes be sold to a small publisher for a lump sum and a royalty arrangement. The advantage here is that you are able to get out from under the work of publicizing it, taking orders, wrapping, shipping, and invoicing, which all consume time that you might prefer to use in other ways.

Successful Spinners

Spinners of various ages, in different parts of the country, in a great variety of situations have found a real market for something they enjoy doing. While many are supplementing their family income, others are earning their entire livelihood with spinning and spinning-related activities. The people described in the following pages represent only a small number of those who are actually earning money with their spinning.

For those who have a reason to contact any of these people, I would like to add a note of caution here: most working craftsmen do not encourage unannounced visitors. Customers should write or call ahead if they would like to visit, unless it is a shop that is open to the public. And it is always appreciated if any mail inquiry is accompanied by a stamped envelope. The cumulative postage for answering these inquiries, over a period of time, can add up to a substantial amount of money.

Priscilla Blosser-Rainey
The River Farm
Route 1, Box 169 A
Timberville, Virginia 22853

Priscilla and her husband, Jerry, farm in the Shenandoah Valley, raising black sheep and selling fleeces to spinners. Priscilla also sells yarn to individuals and shops, at fairs, and by mail order, charging more for two-ply than for one-ply, but spinning several sizes and various plies. Since she has a great selec-

Priscilla Blosser-Rainey skirting fleeces for sale at The River Farm.

tion of fleeces (those from her own sheep and those purchased from neighbors for resale), she has enough prime quality to be able to spin the wool in the grease, just washing the yarn before it is sold. She does feel, however, that her knitted and woven handspun items sell better than yarn, in proportion to the effort put into selling.

She also sells spinning and weaving supplies, wheels, looms, spindles, carders, accessories, and books. Spinning is taught at The River Farm for ten weekends a year, with students signing up for lodging and breakfasts at a nearby inn. Priscilla also teaches at a local college, and gives private weaving lessons. Advertising in *Shuttle Spindle & Dyepot*, *Weaver's Newsletter*, and *Fiberarts* results in steady demand for her fleeces, lessons, and spinning supplies.

Send stamped envelope for price list, $1.00 for sample card.

Allen and Dorothy Fannin
P.O. Box 62
Westdale, New York 13483

The Fannins started in Brooklyn, where their spinning and weaving consisted mainly of large hangings, but sixteen years later in upstate New York, they have shifted to more functional products. In addition to making handspun yarns, they weave scarves, hoods, table mats, coverlets, and yardage, selling both retail and wholesale. Both work at it full time to earn their entire livelihood.

The Fannins emphasize skill, speed, and efficiency. While free-lancing as sample weavers and designers, they learned many mill techniques (such as using dobby heads with up to thirty shafts on their handlooms), which have been incorporated into their process. Power-driven equipment is used for carding, warping, yarn winding, and some handspinning. *Spin-Off* magazine says they are "at the forefront of the modern approach to handspinning."

"Looming Thoughts," which appeared in the 1977 issue of the annual *Spin-Off* publication, was a continuation of the column that was a regular feature in *Handweaver & Craftsman*, for which Mr. Fannin wrote articles on such subjects as hand carding, flax spinning, and repairing spinning wheels.

Dorothy Fannin with sample carder used in wool processing and custom carding.

Allen Fannin spinning needlepoint yarn on automatic spinning machine.

Luisa Gelenter spinning wool on treadle great wheel.

Madelyn Johannes spinning wool on electric spike spinner.

He has written a new book on handloom weaving technology as a sequel to his *Handspinning—Art and Technique*, published in 1970 by Van Nostrand Reinhold. He also has taught many workshops, including ones at Haystack Mountain School of Crafts in Deer Isle, Maine, and at Brookfield Craft Center in Brookfield, Connecticut.

Send stamped envelope for price list of yarn, woven items, and custom carding.

Luisa Gelenter and Madelyn Johannes
La Lana Wools
P.O. Box 2461
Taos, New Mexico 87571

Luisa Gelenter was inspired to learn spinning by seeing spindle spinning being done in South America. She taught Madelyn Johannes and they went into business. Starting with one hundred pounds of white and gray roving and almost no capital, they spent six months spinning and dyeing before offering any of their yarn for sale.

Luisa says they naively thought that an ad in a weaving magazine would do it all for them. As it turned out, it resulted only in orders for their sample cards, probably ordered out of curiosity by other spinners. Since then, however, they have seen their business grow and flourish. They offer white yarn, natural dark yarns, and yarns dyed with both native plants and purchased dyes, such as indigo and cochineal. Although they spin a choice of two yarn sizes, an extra

charge is made for plying, and they sell a minimum order of one pound, with approximately thirty-day delivery. In addition to selling their own dyed yarns, they offer a dyeing service, charging by the pound for dyeing one hundred percent wool yarns provided by the customer.

The wheels they use are unusual, as they are both spindle-type rather than flyer wheels. One is electrically powered and is best for rovings, while the other has a large wheel and a foot treadle and is better for fleece spinning.

Send $3.00 for sample card.

Susan Goldin
Box 411
Stony Brook, New York 11790

Susan Goldin has been spinning for about ten years, sold yarn for a few years, but more recently has been using all her handspun in her own weaving, which is about ninety percent fiber art and ten percent utilitarian pieces. Some of her favorite fibers now are New Zealand fleece carded in the grease, raw uncarded New Zealand fleece, and silk top, but she also uses some rayon and viscose fiber blends. Many of her fibers are used in their natural colors, but some are dyed with vegetable dyes, some with commercial dyes. She uses a drum carder for blending, but uses hand cards or combs on special fibers.

At one time Susan did demonstrations

for a fee, primarily at schools and libraries. Now she teaches both spinning and weaving at the Museums at Stony Brook Craft Center, teaches weaving at a local university, and gives workshops. Since 1974 she has been regularly doing gallery and museum exhibits.

From her studio connected to her home, she sells equipment, fleeces, and books, and also has an annual sale for the public, consisting of her regular work plus a good selection of small items.

Susan organized the Spinning Study Group of Long Island, which meets at the Museums at Stony Brook Craft Center and publishes the *Mother of All News.* She is especially interested in doing yarn design for industry.

No yarn sample card or catalog.

Carol Graham
North Idaho Homespun
Route 1, Box 459
Bonners Ferry, Idaho 83805

North Idaho Homespun was originally a partnership of two young women who used spinning to earn extra income for their families. They lived thirty miles apart, but shared a drum carder and marketed their yarns together, using Carol's address.

Although they spun all sizes of yarn, the most popular was their medium weight two-ply, either vegetable dyed or white. Fleeces were purchased at the spring sheep

Susan Goldin spinning in her home-studio.

Carol Graham displaying her yarn at a craft fair.

shearing at the fairgrounds, with an effort made to convince local sheep raisers that there was a good market for *clean* wool.

They started out by demonstrating and selling at fairs, and signed up interested people for their classes. For spinning, they both had Ashford wheels with the faster whorls, and a jumbo flyer for a third Ashford, used for spinning bulky yarns.

After three years her partner moved away, so Carol is now the sole producer of North Idaho Homespun. She tries to get most of the fleeces spun up during the winter months so she can have a nice stock of yarns to take to craft fairs during the summer.

Send $2.00 (refundable) for sample card.

Bette and Bernard Hochberg
333 Wilkes Circle
Santa Cruz, California 95060

Bette Hochberg has been spinning since childhood, and professionally for about twelve years. She spins many fibers, specializing mostly in fibers other than wool: cotton, linen, silk, cashmere, camel down, alpaca, and mohair. A good stock of these fibers is always kept on hand. Yarns are all one-ply, in natural colors only, with sizes ranging from 8,000 yards per pound in cotton to thick ropy goat hair and camel. Much of the thicker yarn is for her husband's use in rug weaving. Bernard Hochberg has been

weaving rugs for sale for about ten years, using handspun on heavy linen or goat hair warps. Bette's specialty is a pearly gray handspun and handwoven cashmere shawl, twenty-two by eighty-eight inches, weighing four ounces.

Spinning- and weaving-related activities comprise their whole income. Each year they attend one craft fair, a local one in Santa Cruz. There they only sell, and do not demonstrate. The rest of the year is spent filling custom spinning and weaving orders and doing a few gallery exhibits. Bette gives some private lessons to spinning teachers, some classes for a local craft shop, and some advanced spinning workshops for groups, but does not travel to put on workshops. She also has written *Handspinner's Handbook* and *Handspindles*.

No yarn sample card or catalog.

Miranda Howard
Shepherd's Harvest
1925 Central Avenue
Evanston, Illinois 60201

Miranda Howard has been spinning for nine years and selling yarn for over four years. She is a partner in the Shepherd's Harvest in Evanston, where she sells her yarn under the trademarked label of Shepherd Spun. She uses 54s domestic top, selling some of it white and some dyed with cushing dyes, and spins another yarn that is

Bette Hochberg spinning fine linen.

Bernard Hochberg at his rug loom.

Miranda Howard spinning yarn for sale at the Shepherd's Harvest.

Cheri Jensen with one of her dogs, whose fur is used for spinning.

a mixture of wool and camel hair, in natural shades.

Miranda has completely supported herself since 1972 with her spinning, weaving, and teaching. The majority of her income is from teaching spinning and from spinning custom yarns from fibers provided by pet owners. These custom yarns are priced according to the time it takes to spin them. She also spins wool in the grease for weaving of rugs and shawls, and does paid demonstrations and lectures at a museum in Chicago.

The Ashford wheel is her choice for the Shepherd Spun yarns and for teaching, while an Irish wheel is her favorite for custom yarns. Miranda's future plans include writing a specialized book on the properties and proper use of different spinning fibers.

Send stamped envelope for price list, $1.00 for sample card.

Cheri Jensen
Rural Route 3, Box 3109
Juneau, Alaska 99801

Cheri Jensen has been spinning for about eight years, and gradually worked into selling by trading her yarn with other craftsmen and suppliers. One interesting trade was a handspun and knit sweater for a winter's supply of chicken and goat feed. Since she and her husband were building their own two-story stone and log house, her spinning time had been limited until recently. She has been advertising her yarn for sale for over a year now, and spins with an Ashford wheel, which she also uses when teaching.

By mail order, she specializes in custom spinning fibers (most often dog hair) provided by her customers, with prices varying for single-ply, two-ply, and special effects. For an additional fee, the yarn will be knit into hats, mittens, scarves, tunics, shawls, sweaters, and ponchos.

Carding is done with two drum carders, one with medium teeth and one with quite fine teeth. For fine furs that require hand carding, she charges more due to the extra time involved.

Cheri also does some spinning of alpaca, camel, and cashmere, but very little sheep's wool. She expects to offer weaving for sale, also, after she completes the rugs, drapery, and upholstery for their new home.

Send large stamped envelope for price list.

Sachiye Jones
28068 Ham Road
Eugene, Oregon 97405

Sachiye Jones has been spinning for thirteen years, having learned when she and her husband, John, spent three years working in Mexico. On returning to the Northwest, she paid her tuition for graduate studies at the University of Oregon by spinning yarn for sale.

She and her husband live on a large farm, which has good pasture for their Karakul-Romney dark sheep. With seven years of crossbreeding, they have made much improvement in both wool and conformation, and sell breeding stock to other spinners.

Their yarn- and farm-related incomes provide half of their living, with John working also as a carpenter. They do all the farm chores and sheep shearing, and raise the hay they need. The only hired help in the spinning-weaving business is a woman who does the drum carding. Of the yarn that Sachiye spins, half is sold retail by mail order

or through shops. The rest is woven or knitted, and the clothing items—scarves, vests, ponchos, ruanas, and sweaters—are sold through shops.

Sachiye is the founder and editor of the *Black Sheep Newsletter*, a publication for all sheep growers and spinners who are interested in natural colored sheep.

Send large stamped envelope and $1.00 for catalog.

Sachiye Jones teasing wool on the porch of her home-studio.

Annie Kelley
Pennyfield Wool
Pennyfield Lock
Potomac, Maryland 20854

Annie Kelley and her husband, Ridge, have raised sheep for ten years, and Annie has been spinning for nine years. She was already doing some weaving before she learned to spin. Their sheep are mostly purebred red and black Karakuls, whose wool often can be spun without carding, or with minimum use of a flick carder. Her husband does shearing around the area in exchange for wool, which she drum cards for spinning. Some she sells to her students. Any excess is sent to a mill, and the resulting yarn is vegetable dyed for sale and for use in her weaving. She sells the vegetable dyed mill yarn wholesale to thirty shops, and retails her handspun yarn and some woven items. She never sells on consignment.

Annie credits her attractive yarn label, designed by her sister, for an increase in her yarn sales at fairs. There she prices her yarn by the skein rather than by the ounce, and says that a single-ply, overspun, lumpy yarn seems to sell best. She attends several large craft fairs each year, and also gives workshops and paid demonstrations. Home visitors are discouraged, except customers who have made advance arrangements to buy on weekends or at Christmas.

Send stamped envelope for price list, $1.00 for yarn samples.

Annie Kelley with some of her dark ewes.

Christine LeMar
4409 18th Avenue
Kenosha, Wisconsin 53140

Christine LeMar has been spinning nine years, and selling for the last four years, mostly to weavers. She makes multi-ply for her own use, but sells primarily single-ply, through several retail shops and by mail order from her home. Yarn sales provide about half the money she earns, while the rest comes from weaving and toy making.

Christine buys wool from local farmers, as well as by mail. Carding is done on two machines: one is a standard make of drum carder, the other is an electric one with fine carding teeth that was made by Christine's father. Her daughters, Anne Marie and Eleanor, help with the carding and are paid according to how difficult the wool is to tease and how elaborate the color blending is in carding. About seventy percent of the yarns are vegetable dyed, usually in the fleece. Christine, her husband, and the two girls gather the dye plants out in the country.

Christine is a self-taught spinner, and uses an Ashford wheel with a jumbo flyer for spinning wool and mohair, and for plying. She uses a locally made parlor wheel for spinning silk and flax, and a charka for cotton, and also uses an electric spinner. For weaving she uses a forty-eight-inch, four-harness tapestry loom, which her father made, and a forty-eight-inch floor loom.

Send stamped envelope for price list.

Christine LeMar spinning weaving yarn.

Adrienne Shuker Loupos
Agapo
R.D. 1
Temple, Pennsylvania 19560

Adrienne Loupos has been spinning for about five years, using an Ashford wheel for both single and plied yarns. She sells her yarns and weaving, which is done on a forty-eight-inch Macomber loom and a sixty-inch Leclerc loom, at the ten craft fairs she attends. Demonstrations are done on a small Harrisville loom. She finds that selling woven articles is more profitable than just selling yarn. Among her yarn customers are many students from nearby Kutztown State College. From her studio she also sells spinning wheels, looms, books, and some fleeces from her own sheep as well as from local farms.

Since she breeds Shetland sheep dogs for sale, also, it is natural that she utilizes their wool in her work; she spins dog combings provided by her customers, as well. The dog combings are hand carded, spun, then washed gently. The first rinse has lemon juice added to offset the doggy aroma. The last rinse contains a hair conditioner to impart a luster to the yarn.

Adrienne also teaches classes in spinning and in weaving, both at her home-studio and at the YWCA, and demonstrates at the Daniel Boone Homestead.

Send stamped envelope for price list, $1.00 for sample card.

Adrienne Shuker Loupos weaving with handspun.

Winifred M. Poole
Rural Route 1, Box 240
Trafalgar, Indiana 46181

Winifred Poole has been spinning for sixteen years and raising sheep for twenty years, adding dark ones to her flock a few years ago.

She spins all sizes, both one- and two-ply, with most of the yarn sold in her shop, the Wool Skein Sheep Shed on West Washington Street in Nashville, Indiana. It is in a two-story barn, in a complex of ten small shops; here she sells spinning and weaving supplies, pelts, handspun yarn, and items made from handspun. The yarn sales make up about a quarter of her income. Yarn is priced by the yard, which is an unusual way of pricing, but has proven to work best in this area. Single-ply costs the least, two-ply and natural dyed more. In addition, Winifred gives spinning and weaving lessons, and sells both black and white sheep. She goes to art fairs to sell, and demonstrates spinning each year in the Wool Room of the Indiana State Fair sheep barn. Her husband repairs antique wheels.

Send stamped envelope for price list.

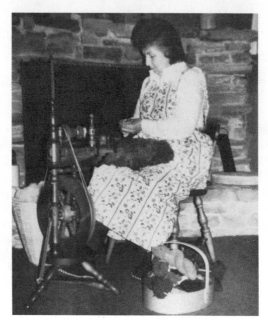

Winifred Poole spinning wool for her shop.

Peter and Helga Reimers
Green Mountain Creative Crafts
Hinesburg, Vermont 05461

Peter Reimers had an industrial background when he and his family settled on an abandoned farm in Vermont. Helga

has been weaving for over thirty years. Her German ancestors were semiprofessional weavers and each piece of her weaving has the old family trademark woven into it. Both Helga and Peter spin, as do their four children. However, their emphasis is on weaving—they started spinning only when they could not find the textured yarns that they prefer for their natural colored weavings. Wool from their own black sheep is used for their yarn, and they also buy wools from around the world, which they wash and then card on a drum carder.

For the last ten years, the Reimers have concentrated on developing their home industry. For a while they sold their handspun yarn, but now they use all of it in their weaving, which they sell at about six of the larger

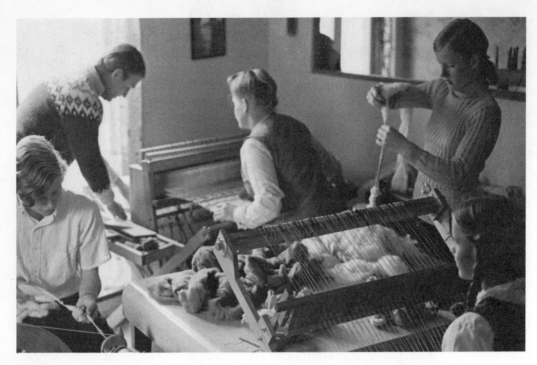

The Reimers family at work.

craft fairs, as well as to some selected stores and by direct mail order. Their pillows sell well by mail.

Most of their income is from selling weavings, fleeces, black sheep breeding stock, maple syrup, and their own looms, which Peter designed. They give week-long weaving classes in the summer for a limited number of students, and short intensive spinning and weaving workshops at their farm in the winter.

Send stamped envelope for price list.

Ginger Shive
The Shearing Shed
P.O. Box 585
Sisters, Oregon 97759

Ginger Shive is so identified with her shop, The Shearing Shed, that it is impossible to tell about her without most of the talk being about her unusual shop.

The business people of the little town of Sisters decided that the town had a basically "western" look of the 1800s, and encouraged the planning commission to decree that any new building or exterior remodeling had to reflect that period. Ginger's building is actually one of the oldest in town, with the original weathered pine exterior and rough pine walls. ("Not a plumb line among them," she says.) The floor is unstained and has used braided rugs on it. Old oak showcases, oval

mirrors, and an antique cash register complete the effect.

Ginger does a good business in spinning supplies and in handwoven garments, many of which are made from handspun yarn. Fleeces and carded wool are stored in bins, along with large quantities of handspun yarn by several northwest spinners. She spins quite a bit of yarn for the shop from her own dark sheep's wool, when she is not submerged in bookkeeping chores. Her load of paper work has been increased because of the purchase of the Fiber Arts Warehouse, which has been moved up to Sisters from New Mexico. Luckily her husband, Bob, approves and encourages her, and his father assists in the complicated accounting problems.

Send large stamped envelope for catalog.

Ginger Shive spinning in her shop.

Christina, Isabel, and Irene Smucker
Smuckers' Cottage Industries
Rural Route 1, Star Route 287
West Liberty, Ohio 43357

The three Smucker sisters earn their complete living from spinning and weaving. Much of their selling is done in a small shop adjoining their home, in a tourist area of Ohio. They also attend one major craft fair per year, the four-day Appalachian Festival in Cincinnati, where they display and take enough orders to last about half of the year.

They spin tapestry yarn from washed, hand carded, and vegetable dyed wool, then weave this into historical scenes, size eighteen by thirty-two inches. They use an Ashford wheel to spin wool, some of it spun in the grease and then washed. They use a castle-type wheel for spinning silk, which is one of the fibers they use in their Sherpa coats, made in several lengths and in small, standard, and large sizes. Customers have four choices of fabric in these coats: silk noil, silk and handspun wool, camel hair and handspun wool, or all wool mill yarn. Borders on the coats are handspun textured braid.

At this time all of their yarn is used to weave coats, tapestries, or fireside rugs, so they are not selling yarn. They have no catalog and do not teach, but do give paid demonstrations by appointment.

Send stamped envelope for price list.

Isabel Smucker spinning in their studio-shop.

Christina Smucker sorting the wool of their ewe Elida.

Irene Smucker spinning dark brown sweater yarn.

Alice Stough
Alice in Wonderland
Route 1, Box 405
Millstone, West Virginia 25261

When Alice and Lee Stough were married ten years ago, they felt that children needed to be raised on a farm and have both parents with them full time. So they gave up their jobs and bought 111 acres—including 8 acres cropland and 15 acres pasture and hay land, mostly red clay. Lee devoted his energy to building up the farm. All that Alice knew how to do at home was knit. She started with commercial yarn, encouraged by the West Virginia Arts and Humanities Council, and began to sell her work. After ordering

some of my handspun, she decided to search for black sheep, and not use machine-spun or dyed yarn. They started out with three black sheep and one white, and have worked up to fifty.

Alice spins mostly a bulky yarn, single-ply. She is a member of the West Virginia Artists and Craftsmans Guild, and her work has the Seal of Quality. In 1978 she was selected as one of the top ten craftsmen in the state. She sells no yarn, but knits all her handspun into sweaters, blankets, shawls, and ponchos, selling them retail at craft fairs.

They have a milk cow, and grow and preserve about eighty percent of all the food for themselves and their three children. An apple orchard of five hundred trees will soon be producing well, and they plan to start selling black sheep breeding stock.

Send stamped envelope for price list.

Kay Thomas
707 Atlantic Avenue
Monaca, Pennsylvania 15061

Kay Thomas has been spinning for sixteen years (after buying a wheel just to use as a decoration) and has been selling yarn for ten years. One outlet in her area is Old Economy Village, where she also demonstrates spinning and weaving. Teaching at a museum and at a craft school takes up much of her time.

One annual demonstration, for which she is paid, is at the Canfield Fair in Ohio. In front of the wool display at the sheep barn,

she spins the grand champion fleece from the previous year, then brings it back the next year, woven into an article for display.

Kay's favorite fleece breed is Cheviot, which she washes and prepares by carding or combing, then spins into fine yarn for plying. The same price is charged for one-ply and two-ply. Ciba-dyed fleeces are blended with a drum carder to achieve the desired shades for her tapestry skeins, used in her own weaving. Handspun is used for both warp and weft in all of her weaving.

Send stamped envelope for price list.

Linda Berry Walker
Woodsedge Farmstead
P.O. Box 464
Kingston, New Jersey 08528

Linda came from Iowa, studied at Arrowmont School in Tennessee, and ended up on a one-hundred-acre farm in New Jersey. Her yarn sales financed the fencing and sheep purchasing, and continue to provide the grain and hay. Her husband makes much of her equipment and is a supportive partner in many ways.

She spins two basic production yarns: a medium thin one-ply used for weaving and crocheting, and a heavier weight two-ply used more for knitting. In addition, she has mohair-wool blends and custom-spun fancy yarns. She retails her natural colored handspun as well as vegetable dyed homespun from her farm workshop, which is a separate building. She also sells nine makes of spin-

Alice Stough with knitted craft fair items.

Kay Thomas demonstrating and exhibiting her weaving.

Linda Berry Walker stoking the fire under a dye pot.

Jean Woodward with yarn in her home-studio.

ning wheels and other spinning and weaving equipment, plus a great variety of fleeces and fibers.

Linda gives lectures, paid demonstrations, and workshops, such as one on "Wool Awareness," showing wool of seventy different breeds from around the world and discussing their special qualities.

She takes two apprentices each year, from about May through October. They train in various processes for six weeks, then stay on and do the drum carding and other chores for five months. The apprentices also attend all her workshops free, as assistants.

She is active in the New Jersey Designer Craftsmen organization and books many of their lecturers, who are spinning and weaving experts from around the country.

Send long stamped envelope for price list, $2.00 for samples.

Jean Woodward
Hemlock Hill Handspinners
28405 Honeysuckle Drive
Damascus, Maryland 20750

Jean Woodward has been spinning for seven years, teaching for three years, and selling her yarn for about two years, with the help of two daughters who spin and also care for their small flock of sheep and Angora rabbits.

Most of her classes are taught through the County Recreational Program, which handles the promotion as well as the signing up of students, with classes held in the Woodward home. Jean charges a fee plus a charge for supplies and use of equipment. A separate studio room is used, which has eight different wheels plus other equipment. Private lessons are offered, also.

Several craft fairs provide a market for Jean's yarn and finished items, such as mittens, shawls, and hats; some of these are spun of wool, some of dog hair, and some of angora. Additional income comes from selling spinning wheels, carders, spindles, and books from her home-studio, where customers come by appointment. She does not plan to have a retail shop, saying that the rent would eat up the profit.

Send stamped envelope for price list, $1.00 for samples.

Sources

Fleeces

Listed in "Sources" chapter of *Spinning and Weaving with Wool.*

Centrifugal Extractors

Listed in telephone directory's "Yellow Pages" under "Laundry Equipment."

Hand Wringer

Countryside
Route 1
Waterloo, Wisconsin 53594

Sears, Roebuck and Company
Listed under "Clothes Wringers" in catalog.

Wool Teaser-Picker (Large)

Carl Goldscheider
General Delivery
Merville, British Columbia
Canada V0R 2M0

Cradle Picker, Made to Order

Levi Ross Custom Woodwork
P.O. Box 506
Chimacum, Washington 98325

Wool Duster, General Plans

Lorraine Wells
18728 Southeast Cheldelin Road
Portland, Oregon 97236

Wool Hand Combs, Wool Hackle

Eliza Leadbeater
Rookery Cottage
Dalesfords Lane
Whitegate, Northwich
Cheshire, England CW8 2BN

Custom Carding Services

Baron Woolen Mills
P.O. Box 340
Brigham City, Utah 84302
801-734-9436
Cards into roving and sliver only. Minimum 100 lb. to get own wool returned.

Bartlettyarns
Harmony, Maine 04942
207-683-2251
No minimum on washed wool, own wool returned. Minimum of 100 lb. grease wool to be washed, carded, and returned. Can card into 1-in. rolags or ¼-in. pencil roving. Can handle Karakul, but not Merino.

Birkland Brothers Wool Batts
3573 Main Street
Vancouver, British Columbia
Canada V5V 3N4
604-874-5734
Clean washed fleeces, minimum 4 lb. Deals by mail; payments must be by postal money order only.

Courtenay Carding
Rural Route 2, Condensory Road
Courtenay, British Columbia
Canada V9N 5M9
604-338-8224
Cards, and can do worsted carding into sliver. Minimum about 6 lb.

Everton Mattress Company
24 East 1st South Street
Brigham City, Utah 84302
801-723-6431
Clean washed wool only, minimum 5 lb.

Allen Fannin
P.O. Box 62
Westdale, New York 13483
315-245-2887
Clean fleeces only, no minimum. Cards short and medium-short wools.

Harrisville Designs
Harrisville, New Hampshire 03450
603-827-3334
No minimum on washed fleeces. Can scour in 100-lb. quantities.

Kukowski Woolen Mills
Route 3
Winona, Minnesota 55987
Send stamped envelope for information. Has backlog of carding orders. Will accept and return by mail. No minimum on wool. Can also wash fleeces.

Lambing Valley Farm
Janet Sorrels
Beatty Run Road
Franklin, Pennsylvania 16323
814-374-4281
Call or send stamped envelope for information. Clean washed wool only.

Northwest Wool Company
4609 14th Northwest
Seattle, Washington 98107
206-783-6911
Washed wool only, minimum 3 lb. Cards into batts. Will accept and return by mail.

Old Sturbridge Village
Sturbridge, Massachusetts 01566
617-347-3362
Shipper must have advance written reservation and acceptance before sending wool. Washed wool only, no more than 25 lb. in a shipment.

Potrero Woolworks
El Rito, New Mexico 87530
Minimum 3 to 5 lb., accepted and returned by mail.

Saint Peter Woolen Mills
Saint Peter, Minnesota 56082
507-931-3702
Clean washed wool only, minimum 3 lb.

Shippensburg Woolen Mill
Alma Van Scyoc
13 North Washington Street
Shippensburg, Pennsylvania 17257
717-532-6211
*Very clean washed wool only. Minimum 5 lb.,
accepted and returned by mail.*

Wausau Woolen Company
408 South 4th Street
Wausau, Wisconsin 54401
715-848-9293
*Washed wool, or can do washing; 7 lb. grease
wool is about 3 lb. carded.*

Lorraine Wells
18728 Southeast Cheldelin Road
Portland, Oregon 97236
503-665-6396
*Very clean washed fleeces only, no minimum.
Will card quantities as small as 3 lb. and
still return your wool. By mail, or done
while you wait (by appointment only).*

**Carding and Spinning Oil, Wholesale
and Retail**

Obadiah Tharp Company
8406 Southwest 58th Avenue
Portland, Oregon 97219

Foot-Powered Drum Carder

John and Sachiye Jones
28068 Ham Road
Eugene, Oregon 97405

**Custom Spinning of "Homespun-Type"
Yarn from Customer's Fleeces**

Bartlettyarns
Harmony, Maine 04942

Harrisville Designs
Harrisville, New Hampshire 03450

Motorized Bulk Spinners

Ernest Mason
3033 Northeast Davis Street
Portland, Oregon 97232

Sam Noto
6504 39th Avenue
Kenosha, Wisconsin 53142

John White
39918 North Ruby Road
Scio, Oregon 97374

Treadle Automatic Spinners

Bud Kronenberg
Horse Fence Hill Road
Southbury, Connecticut 06488

Felix Stephens
14997 240th Street East
Graham, Washington 98338

Electric Spinners

Alden Amos
c/o Straw into Gold
5533 College Avenue
Oakland, California 94618

Clemes and Clemes
650 San Pablo Avenue
Pinole, California 94564
Shown on page 86 of Spinning and Weaving
with Wool.

Crisp Woodworking Concern
333 Southeast 3d
Portland, Oregon 97214

Greentree Ranch
163 North Carter Lake Road
Loveland, Colorado 80537
Kircher distributor.

Firma Kircher
Alte Kasseler Str. 24
Postfech 1408
Marburg, West Germany

Plix Products
P.O. Box 944
Hastings, New Zealand

Nakui Seisakusho
No. 17, 2-Chome Ueda
Morioka-shi, Japan
Correspondence must be in Japanese.

Yarn Blocker Plans

Blocker plans are shown in *Spinning and
Weaving with Wool*, or send a long
stamped envelope and 25¢ to Paula
Simmons, Box 12, Suquamish,
Washington 98392.

The horizontal warping reel in *Spinning and
Weaving with Wool* can be built in
miniature to be about 1½ yd. in
diameter, with a handle on one end
of the axle, and used as a folding yarn
blocker.

McMorran Yarn Balance

Grandor Industries
P.O. Box 5831
Sherman Oaks, California 91403

Large Free-Standing Yarn Skeiner

Obadiah Tharp Company
8406 Southwest 58th Avenue
Portland, Oregon 97219

Large Free-Standing Squirrel Cage Swift

Lathe & Loom
Thomas Noble
1218 North 46th
Seattle, Washington 98103

Custom Weaving Service

Allen Fannin
P.O. Box 62
Westdale, New York 13483
Weaving done to order with your yarn.

Fly Shuttle Looms

Mailes Looms
4620 Glen Haven Road
Soquel, California 95073
Widths of 48 and 64 in.

Warp Sizing, Retail

Obadiah Tharp Company
8406 Southwest 58th Avenue
Portland, Oregon 97219

Oldebrook Spinnery
Mountain Road
Lebanon, New Jersey 08833

Robin and Russ Handweavers
533 North Adams Street
McMinnville, Oregon 97128

Serendipity Shop
1523 Ellinwood
Des Plaines, Illinois 60016

Also sold at most spinning and weaving
shops. Sizing process is described
in detail in *Spinning and Weaving
with Wool.*

Warp Sizing, Wholesale

Paula Simmons
Box 12
Suquamish, Washington 98392

Ball Winders for Yarn

School Products Company
1201 Broadway
New York, New York 10001

Hobby Knit (Automatic Knitter of Tubular Cord)

Nasco
Craft Catalog
Fort Atkinson, Wisconsin 53538

Woven Labels

Alfa Fabric Label Company
1422 K Street Northwest
Washington, D.C. 20005

Alkahn Labels
70 West 40th Street
New York, New York 10018

Anchor Woven Label Company
10 West 33d Street
New York, New York 10001

Anderman Tag and Label
225 West 34th Street
New York, New York 10001

Applebaum Tag and Label Company
30-30 Northern Boulevard
Long Island City, New York 11101

Aragon Woven Label
1582 Atlantic Avenue
Brooklyn, New York 11213

Artistic Identification Systems
c/o Don Adams Company
9010 North Decatur
Portland, Oregon 97203

Auburn Label and Tag Company
10 West 33d Street
New York, New York 10001

Label Weave
450 7th Avenue
New York, New York 10001

Supreme Label Corporation
109 West 27th Street
New York, New York 10001

U.S. Woven Label Company
205 West 34th Street
New York, New York 10001

Warner Artex
111 West 40th
New York, New York 10018

Wovencraft Label Service
450 7th Avenue
New York, New York 10001

See also "Labels, woven" in telephone directory's "Yellow Pages."

Address Labels (Paper)

Walter Drake and Sons
94 Drake Building
Colorado Springs, Colorado 80940

Partial Listing of Regularly Scheduled Workshops

Albion Hills Farm School of Spinning, Dyeing and Weaving
Edna Blackburn
Rural Route 3
Caledon East, Ontario
Canada L0N 1E0

Arrowmont School of Crafts
Box 567
Gatlinburg, Tennessee 37738

Bonneville Gallery and Loom Room
P.O. Box 32
Gig Harbor, Washington 98335

Damascus School for Pioneer Crafts
14711 Southeast Anderson Road
Clackamas, Oregon 97015

Fletcher Farm Craft School
Ludlow, Vermont 05149

Hambridge Center
P.O. Box 33
Rapun Gap, Georgia 30568

Jones Sheep Farm
Marilyn Jones
Route 2, Box 185
Peabody, Kansas 66866

The Mannings
Creative Crafts
Route 2
East Berlin, Pennsylvania 17316

Oldebrook Spinnery
Mountain Road
Lebanon, New Jersey 08833

Pacific Basin Textile Arts
P.O. Box 7033
Berkeley, California 94707

Hal Painter
Star Route 2, Box 570 D
Chiloquin, Oregon 97624

Pendleton Fabric Craft School
Mary Pendleton
Box 233, Jordan Road
Sedona, Arizona 86336

The River Farm
Priscilla Blosser-Rainey
Route 1, Box 169 A
Timberville, Virginia 22853

Weavers Guild of Minnesota
2402 University Avenue
Saint Paul, Minnesota 55114

Woodsedge Farmstead
Linda Berry Walker
P.O. Box 464
Kingston, New Jersey 08528

Related Reading

The Crafts Business Encyclopedia
by Michael Scott
New York: Harcourt Brace Jovanovich, 1977

The Craftsman's Survival Manual
by George and Nancy Wettlaufer
Englewood Cliffs, New Jersey:
    Prentice-Hall, 1974

Craftsmen in Business
by Howard W. Connaughton, C.P.A.
Publication of American Crafts Council
44 West 53d Street
New York, New York 10019

Felt Making for the Fiber Artist
by Louise Green
Greentree Ranch
163 North Carter Lake Road
Loveland, Colorado 80537

Getting Published: An Author's Guide to Book Publishing
by David St. John and Hubert Bermont
New York: Harper & Row Publishers, 1973

The Literary Agent
Free from Society of Authors'
    Representatives
101 Park Avenue
New York, New York 10017

Patterns for Handspun
by Paula Simmons
Box 12
Suquamish, Washington 98392
Send $1.35 plus postage

Profitable Craft Merchandising
Peoria, Illinois: PJS Publications, 1977

Raising Sheep the Modern Way
by Paula Simmons
Charlotte, Vermont: Garden Way Publish-
    ing, 1976

Small Business Administration
    pamphlets
Free advice for small businesses
P.O. Box 15434
Fort Worth, Texas 96119

Spinning and Weaving with Wool
by Paula Simmons
Seattle: Pacific Search Press, 1977

Tax Guide for Small Businesses
IRS publication #334
Free from Internal Revenue Service

Publications

Artisan Crafts
Box 398
Libertyville, Illinois 60048

Black Sheep Newsletter
28068 Ham Road
Eugene, Oregon 97405

The Crafts Report
(includes *The Working Craftsman*)
P.O. Box 1992
Wilmington, Delaware 19899

Fiberarts
50 College Street
Asheville, North Carolina 28801

Goodfellow Review of Crafts
P.O. Box 4520
Berkeley, California 94704

Interweave
2938 North County Road 13
Loveland, Colorado 80537

The Looming Arts
P.O. Box 233
Sedona, Arizona 86336

Mother of All News
Spinning Study Group of Long Island
Museums at Stony Brook Craft Center
Christian Avenue
Stony Brook, New York 11790

Naturally
Gordon's Naturals
P.O. Box 506
Roseburg, Oregon 97470

Shuttle Spindle & Dyepot
998 Farmington Avenue
West Hartford, Connecticut 06107

Spin-Off (annual)
2938 North County Road 13
Loveland, Colorado 80537

Textile Artists Newsletter
5533 College Avenue
Oakland, California 94618

Warp and Weft
533 North Adams
McMinnville, Oregon 97128

Weaver's Newsletter
P.O. Box 259
Homer, New York 13077

U.S. and Metric Measurements

Measurements in *The Handspinner's Guide to Selling* are given in the U.S. form of measurement. Those who prefer to use the metric system will find the following conversion table useful:

inches × 25   = millimeters
inches ×   2.5 = centimeters
feet   × 30   = centimeters
feet   ×   0.3 = meters

10 millimeters (mm) = 1 centimeter (cm)
10 centimeters (cm) = 1 decimeter (dm)
10 decimeters (dm)   = 1 meter (m)

Index

Boldface numerals indicate pages on
which photos or illustrations appear.

Other Books from Pacific Search Press